The Horse's Mind

The Horse's Mind

Lucy Rees

Stanley Paul
London Melbourne Auckland Johannesburg

Stanley Paul & Co. Ltd

An imprint of Century Hutchinson Ltd
Brookmount House, 62–65 Chandos Place, Covent Garden, London WC2N 4NW

Century Hutchinson Australia (Pty) Ltd
PO Box 496, 16–22 Church Street, Hawthorn, Melbourne, Victoria 3122

Century Hutchinson New Zealand Limited
191 Archers Road, PO Box 40-086, Glenfield, Auckland 10

Century Hutchinson South Africa (Pty) Ltd
PO Box 337, Bergvlei 2012, South Africa

First published 1984
Reprinted 1984, 1985, 1986, 1987
© Lucy Rees 1984

Set in Bembo

Printed and bound in Great Britain by Butler & Tanner Ltd,
Frome and London

British Library Cataloguing in Publication Data
Rees, Lucy
    The horse's mind.
    1. Horses - Behaviour
    2. Horse-training
    I. Title
    636.1   SF281

ISBN 0 09 153660 X

Contents

Horses' Hoofs

Horses have hoofs to carry them over frost and snow; hair, to protect them from wind and cold. They eat grass and drink water, and fling up their heels over the champaign. Such is the real nature of horses. Palatial dwellings are of no use to them.

One day Poh Loh appeared saying, 'I understand the management of horses.'

So he branded them, and clipped them, and pared their hoofs, and put halters on them, tying up their heads and shackling their feet, and keeping them in stables, with the result that two or three in every ten died. Then he kept them hungry and thirsty, trotting them and galloping them, and grooming them and trimming them, with the misery of the tasselled bridle before and the fear of the knotted whip behind, until more than half of them were dead.

The potter says, 'I can do what I want with clay. If I want it round I use compasses; if rectangular, a square.'

The carpenter says, 'I can do what I will with wood. If I want it curved I use an arc; if straight, a line.'

But on what grounds can we think that the natures of clay and wood desire this application of compasses and square, of arc and line? Nevertheless, every age extols Poh Loh for his skill in managing horses, and potters and carpenters for their skill with clay and wood . . . .

Horses live on dry land, eat grass and drink water. When pleased, they rub their necks together. When angry, they turn round and kick up their heels at each other. Thus far only do their natural dispositions carry them. But bridled and bitted, with a plate of metal on their foreheads, they learn to cast vicious looks, to turn the head to bite, to resist, to get the bit out of the mouth or the bridle into it. And thus their natures become depraved – the fault of Poh Loh.

(Chuang Tzu, c. 300–400 BC,
translated by Herbert Giles)

Foreword

by Harry Llewellyn

The Welsh have a close affinity with horses because they are so much part of our lives, and I find myself greatly privileged to be asked to write a foreword to this book by Lucy Rees.

I have recorded elsewhere how Foxhunter, my showjumper, who clearly loved showjumping, could read my mind and I could read his. If I wanted him to stop I hardly had to do anything. He just knew what I was *thinking*. There was no question of any severe pulls on the rein. Part of this was due to his cool mind, but one has to realize that all horses have different characters just as humans do. Foxhunter looked upon everybody as a friend and would never think of kicking at anything, even an old lady hugging his leg after a competition. Other horses would lash out.

The causes, for instance, of excitability and irritation in horses can, with care and attention, be avoided. There are some horses whose minds work like tops which spin at increasing speed, causing them to lose the powers of deduction which they certainly have, but this can similarly apply to people. Over-anxiety causes people to make mistakes and again this is the same with horses. If someone rattles the bars of a horsebox, it is not surprising that the horse should get irritated.

Basically a good relationship between man and horse demands sympathy and understanding; those of us living amongst ponies and horses are able to see their point of view. Horses in turn are quick to appreciate this and respond warmly. The domesticated horse has learned to live harmoniously with human beings even if they recognize the power of authority. If a horse is over-dominated, he will hate to go about his business, whether it is pulling a cart or performing over obstacles in competitions. I often wonder how it has come about that horses are so generous in their attitude.

People who fail with horses do so because they do not understand them, and here we come to the importance of this new book. Not only is the author extremely perceptive, but her text gives just the guidance that is needed to develop a true appreciation of the horse's mind. Lucy Rees' book fills a gap and is a valuable contribution towards a fuller understanding of our equine friends.

I hope that thousands will read it carefully and learn from it.

H.L.
Llanvair Grange, 1983

It is a general received opinion, that all this visible world was created for Man; that Man is the End of Creation; as if there were no other end of any creature, but some way or another to be serviceable to man. . . . But though this be vulgarly received, yet wise men now-a-days think otherwise. Dr Moore affirms, that creatures are made to enjoy themselves as well as to serve us.

(John Ray, c. 1690)

Introduction

There are hundreds of books about horses, books about conformation, about riding, training, showing, jumping, driving, breeding, managing, buying, doctoring, feeding, keeping . . . and hundreds more too. There are remarkably few about what goes on in their heads.

This book is about the way that horses behave. But, you may object, they don't all behave the same. Although that is true, the differences in their behaviour are no greater than the differences in their looks, and nobody has any difficulty in recognizing any of them as horses. They are definitely not cows or dogs. They don't behave like cows or dogs either. Nor do they behave like people. However much we try to make them, they do not *think* like us. They see the world differently.

This is not because they are stupid. Horses know what they like and what they do not like, and they move towards the one as surely as they move away from the other. That is not stupid. From their point of view, they behave logically and sensibly.

To us, theirs is an alien logic, just as ours is to them, but whereas they can only remain trapped in their point of view, our gifts of intelligence and imagination make it possible for us to bridge the gap of understanding and to learn their language and thoughts. Without that understanding, we cannot hope to deal with them without creating unhappiness on both sides.

There is a great deal to learn, and in this book I have collected other people's observations freely in an attempt to set down what scientists would call an 'ethogram': a description of the mind and behaviour of the horse like the descriptions of anatomy that others have done. In particular I have gleaned the results of years of work by patient scientists who simply sat and watched horses and then tested their ideas carefully, for it is surely time that their work became available to the rest of the horse world. Some of it, I fear, makes difficult reading: in particular, Chapter 3, which summarizes the general principles of animal behaviour as we understand them at present, may be heavy going. It is perfectly possible to understand the rest of the book without reading that chapter, but I felt it necessary to set it down because interested readers will find that these general principles will help them to understand some behaviour patterns I may not have mentioned.

I could not have written this book without the help I have had from many people (and horses, for that matter). I would like to thank them for their generosity, encouragement and experience and in particular: Dr Mart Kiley-Worthington, whose work on communication has not been fully acknowledged in that section for fear of repetition; Starr Bennett, whose enthusiasm and handsome Morgans (Bill Bailey, Beaming Sun, Shaker-town and Wild Bill) proved so irresistible in the Arizona sun; Seamus Hayes, who taught me so much; Chris Davis, Fred Frye, Carl Satterfield and Mrs Bazy Tankersley, Al-Marah stud, all of Tucson; Dr William Jones, Temecula, California; John Owen, Trawsfynydd; Pamela Price, Nantmor; Professor Jacob Sivak; Dr Jim Lees, Aberystwyth; Professor Angus Graham; Dominic Prince; Dr Tim Clutton-Brock; The Hon. Mrs Moyra Williams; Sheila Gann; D. W. Harwood, Manchester University; and many others whose discussions proved invaluable.

Sara Platt's careful drawings were done from photographs which, for one reason or another, were unsuitable for reproduction.

1
Why a horse looks like he does: a Summary

STAYING ALIVE

In the struggle for life it is, as Darwin described, the fittest that survive. But what is 'fit'? A trout in a river is superbly fit, streamlined and wary; but on the bank it is lamentably not. A mouse skipping in the grass beside the river is fit, but if it falls in the river it becomes hopelessly unfit. An animal's fitness, then, depends on where it is.

Adaptation is the name for the way that animals and plants are suited to their surroundings and their particular way of life. The key to adaptation lies in the environment that the animal or plant lives in: its *habitat*.

Environment

climate + **geology**
(temperature, (type of rock: hard, soft,
rainfall, acid, base, mineral
seasonal changes) content)

give rise to

geography (erosion + **other life forms** (as
patterns: hills, plains, in jungle, tundra, coral
rivers, deserts, etc.) reef, swamp)

Which of the other life forms can be eaten or used in other ways?
Which of them will eat you, or compete for food?

Some habitats are huge: the blue whale's covers half the globe. Others, such as that of the horse louse, are small and restricted. Each presents its own demands, which are met by the animal's adaptation.

How do we recognize adaptation? We classify animals and plants into groups according to their similarities and differences because within each

group we can recognize a basic design, a 'ground plan'. Adaptations mould that ground plan into different forms fitted to certain habitats.

Consider, for a moment, the design of automobiles. The ground plan of an automobile includes some kind of engine, a frame to support it, a way of steering, a place for the driver, and wheels or some other way of moving. Within the group are cars, motorcycles, trucks, vans, caterpillar tractors, etc., each of which has further specifications. None of these is *the* 'ground plan' automobile: all are adapted to some particular job.

In the same way there is no ground plan bird, but all birds have two eyes, two wings, two legs, feathers and a beak; they are warm-blooded and lay eggs. If we look, for instance, at beaks we can see literally hundreds of different adaptations of shape, depending on the bird's food.

A FIT ANIMAL

Given any habitat, we might be able to make reasonable guesses as to what type of animal would best be fitted to live there, and what adaptations might be helpful to its ground plan.

Consider, for example, a large plant-eater (browser/grazer) somewhere on the rolling plains in the temperate zone of the northern hemisphere.

What type of animal could live here? The temperature range means that any large animal must be warm-blooded (*homoiothermic*). Cold-blooded

Figure 1 Birds' beaks *come in different shapes and sizes according to what they are used for, showing the idea of adaptation vividly. Clockwise from top left:*
Bullfinch's *stout, strong little beak snips off buds and fruit and crushes them.*
Crossbill's *strong 'hooks' winkle out seed from pine cones.*
Flower-piercer's *hooked beak is for piercing the base of flowers.*
Nightjar *has a minute beak but an enormous gape. It flies with its mouth open catching flying insects.*
Barn owl's *small hooked beak stabs and tears at small animals.*
Red-breasted merganser's *bill has fringed edges for filtering out tiny organisms from water like a colander.*
Toucan's *vast bill gobbles up mushy fruit, but it does seem extravagantly big even for that.*
Humming-bird's *thin tube sucks up nectar from the base of flowers.*
Golden eagle's *savagely curved beak is ideal for tearing meat (compare with the canine teeth of meat-eating mammals).*
Avocet's *strangely upturned beak is for dragging out and catching small animals at the edge of the tide.*
Puffin's *big bill is for catching fish and bringing them home.*

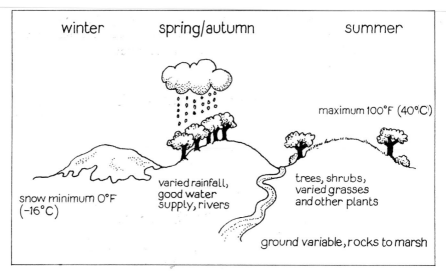

Figure 2 *Rolling plains of North America.*

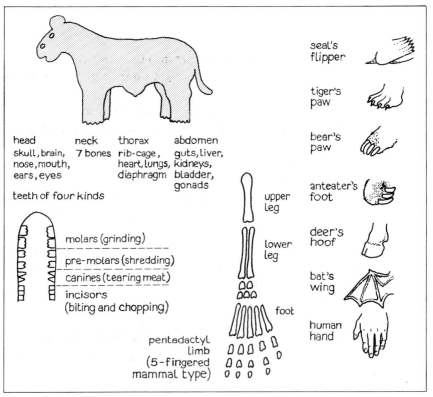

Figure 3 *Ground plan of a mammal (female) (backbone, four legs, warm-blooded, hairy, bearing live young and suckling them).*

(*poikilothermic*) animals would have a hard time surviving in such winters, being too cold to move; they can only grow to a reasonable size in warmer areas. Therefore we might expect to find a mammal.

ADAPTAMAMMAL

For that plain ... as a browser/grazer

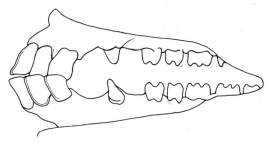

Figure 4 *Horse's teeth.*

Head: long, so that the grass does not get into the eyes when eating.

Teeth: does not need canines (not a meat-eater) but does need good croppers and grinders.

Nose: good at telling the difference between different plants.

Eyes: found high up, above the grass level, and on the sides of the head for good all-round vision. (Unlike hunters or tree-dwellers, this animal does not need much binocular vision as it does not need to be able to judge distances very accurately.)

Ears: right on top of the head, like most mammals; funnel-shaped for good sound collection, and lined with fur so that they do not collect seeds, flies or rain.

Neck: long and flexible for reaching trees. The huge jugular vein, which collects blood from the head, will run down the lower side of the neck, and the longer the neck the greater the heat loss from the vein. An extra layer of insulation (mane) prevents this.

Thorax: deep, to allow for big lungs and heart.

Legs: long, to raise the body above the grass when meandering or running.

Abdomen: generous. Plants take a lot of digesting, and plant-eaters need a big gut packed with bacteria.

Tail: plenty, for warmth in winter and a flywhisk in summer.

Teats: warmer, and more protected, between the back legs.

Coat: plenty in winter, less in summer.

Feet: hard, for wandering over varied ground – hoofs, in fact, for claws
   (good for catching things, or digging) are not necessary.
With these adaptations, the ground-plan mammal becomes something like
this:

Figure 5 *Horse and wolf.*

DANGER: This animal has no defence system, and grass-eaters taste
good ....
EXTRA SURVIVAL PRESSURE ON: sensitive ears; movement-sensitive eyes
(see next chapter); long legs for fast escape, and extra lung and heart space.

Leg adaptations

The fastest-moving part of the leg is the foot, so the lighter the foot the
less the energy needed to move it. By reducing the number of toes and
having one single stout cannon-bone (stronger than several bones of equal
cross-sectional area) horses have evolved the ultimate in speedy legs. Most
hoofed mammals stop at the two-toed stage.
   As in all hoofed mammals, the horse's powerful leg muscles are concentrated high up so that the weight of the moving part of the leg is as small
as possible. The upper bones of the leg are folded up like a concertina,

giving huge extension and a long running stride. This leg and foot arrangement means that the feet can no longer be used for scratching or removing flies over large sections of the body: hence the importance of forelock, tail, and wiggly skin.

Of course, horse evolution did not occur in this simple, all-at-once fashion. It took millions of years for these adaptations to be perfected. Nevertheless it is striking how well-designed horses are for their natural habitat. The success of mustangs and brumbies, both of which arose from escaped horses that had been bred under domestication for hundreds of years, is good proof of this.

2

Sense Organs

Like the rest of his body, a horse's sense organs are strikingly well adapted for the kind of life he should lead.

EYES

With eyes on the sides of his head, a horse can see almost all round himself, though he has a blind zone behind him and also a little way in front of his head.

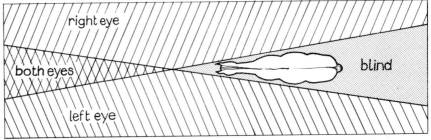

Figure 6 *Blind zone from above.*

The blind zone in front means that if you walk straight towards a horse you disappear when you are right in front of him. To keep you in his sight (which he will want to do unless he knows you well or likes the look of you) he will either turn his head away or walk backwards. Either of these movements is likely to be interpreted as 'not wanting to be caught'. Approaching from an angle keeps you in the horse's view all the time; when you are still a little distance away he may choose to swing his head to face you to get a binocular (two-eyed) view.

The blind zone extends for as much as six feet in front of the horse (it depends slightly on the setting of the eyes: some are positioned so that the horse has better vision forwards). This is perhaps the reason why occasionally in the show ring a horse will cannon straight into a jump 'as if he had not seen it'. The horse is usually jumping a memory, and if he is distracted at the vital moment he may forget where the jump is. Again, this depends a little on the setting of the eyes and, of course, on the position of the horse's head as he is approaching the jump. It is noticeable that most horses tip their heads sideways a little on the approach.

Unless they are both relaxed and aware of what is going on, horses dislike moving objects in the rear blind zone, and turn either their whole bodies or just their heads to see the intruders better. Any movement in this zone may be regarded as a threat particularly by an unhandled, or green, horse. In such cases if the horse cannot move away or turn his head he is liable to kick in what he thinks is self-defence.

Focusing

Horses appear to have little ability to focus by changing the shape or position of the lens as other animals do, and it was thought that they focused on near or far objects by moving their heads up and down so that the image was thrown higher or lower on a ramped retina. (Briefly, it was thought that the retina sloped so that the bottom of it was nearer the lens than the top. Thus, distant objects would be in focus when they were high in the visual field, while near objects would be in focus when low down, *see Smyth, 1974*.) However, more recent anatomical research has shown that the ramp does not exist. Instead what is found is that in the upper and lower extremes of the visual field horses are long-sighted, whereas in the centre their eyes are focused at middle-near distance. In this central area of

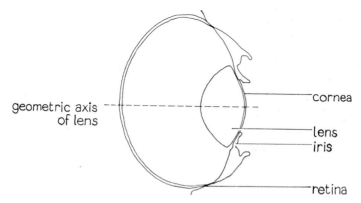

Figure 7 *Vertical section through a horse's eye, traced from a photograph by Sivak.*

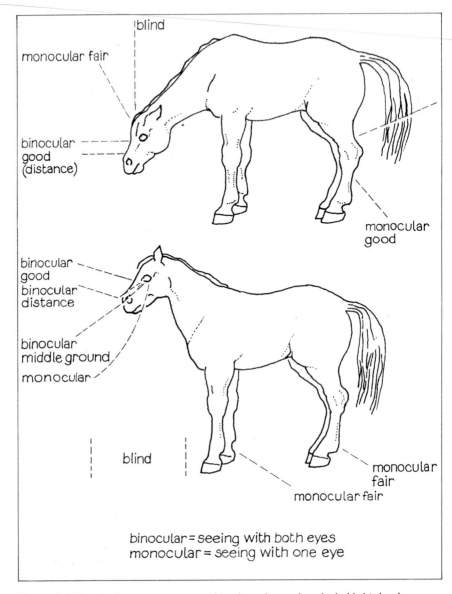

binocular = seeing with both eyes
monocular = seeing with one eye

Figure 8 *What the horse can see around him depends on where he holds his head.*

the retina vision is more detailed, for there is a greater concentration of
visual cells. In all parts of the field, though, the horse's eye is extremely
sensitive to movement. Finally, the visual field of each eye is not round as
ours is, but much wider and less deep, rather like a cinemascope screen
extending almost all round the body.

What all this means is that horses do have to move their heads up and
down, both in order to focus and also to be able to see at all through the

Plate 1 *Quarter horse stallion Conrad Baron, a 'trail horse' competition champion, skilfully negotiates difficult obstacles with ease, his head movements unrestrained by his rider, Carl Satterfield. Walking through the spokes (A) his head is low: he is watching his front feet. Sidepassing over the bar (B), he holds his head higher and watches his side. Backing through the L (C) he drops his head and turns it so that he can see his hocks. His exceptionally prominent eyes (D) make it easy for him to see behind him: compare the setting of his eyes to, say, Beaming Sun's (page 24).*

A

B

C

D

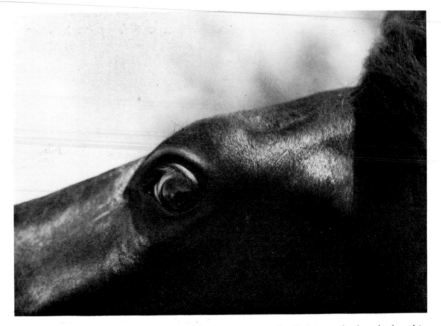

Plate 2 *Beaming Sun, a Morgan colt, raises his nose and rolls his eye back to look at his left hock. Showing the white of the eye is not necessarily a sign of viciousness or temper: it merely shows that the horse is trying to look behind him. The reasons for this can be numerous. When a horse starts to run away from something that has frightened him he often tips his nose up at this angle and rolls his eye to look back, as if to make sure there are no wolves at his heels.*

slit-like pupil. They can do this by rolling their eyes too, though they cannot roll them as much as we can. When a movement in a less-sensitive part of the field attracts their attention they are likely to: EITHER swing the head round to see the thing with both eyes; OR, tilt the head or move it up or down to put the image on a suitable place in the retina; OR, if they cannot or do not want to move the head, roll the eye for the same reason.

A horse with his head high cannot see the ground in front of him, and on rough ground many horses are reluctant to move unless they are given the freedom to drop their heads and look where they are going. Similarly they may be afraid to back in narrow spaces (out of a long trailer, for instance) unless they can see behind them, which they can do EITHER by raising the head high, tipping the nose up and sideways, and rolling the eye, OR by dropping the head, turning it slightly and rolling the eye, when they can see their back feet. When moving they can see even less clearly than when standing still, and young horses often want to stop and look at strange things; if they are not allowed to they may well get panicky. When handling or riding horses we do better by remembering the differences between their eyes and ours.

Figure 9 *Looking at things on the ground. The horse on the left lowers his head to focus on the object; the middle horse, whose object is a bit closer, keeps his eye at the same distance from it as the first horse, so he has to tilt his head to focus. The third horse, whose head is vertical, cannot focus on the object unless he skips sideways (shying) so that the light from the object is coming into his eye at the right angle.*

Figure 10 *Horse walking on hillside.*

A horse walking across a hillside keeps her head at right angles to the ground, so that both uphill and downhill sides are equally in focus.

It has been suggested that frightened horses become more long-sighted because of the action of adrenalin on the eye, though whether this is true or not is uncertain. When afraid, horses raise their heads and stiffen their necks (*see page 155*) so that they cannot see the low foreground anyway.

To focus on objects close beside them, horses must EITHER keep their heads low OR, if their heads are high, tilt them sideways. If this tilting is prevented for instance in a ridden horse, she will have to skip sideways to get further away and reduce the degree of tilting. This action ('spooking' or 'shying') is often punished by riders, either deliberately or by mistake by loss of balance and snatching at the reins. The horse then learns that such objects are likely to hurt and that they should be avoided even more quickly next time.

Colour vision

By teaching horses to go to different coloured buckets, Grzimek showed that they could distinguish yellows, greens and blues well. At the ends of the spectrum – the reds and purples – they could not tell the difference between colours and shades of grey. But more recent Russian research (*see page 29*) shows that they seem to be able to see purples and reds as well.

Since our eyes work so differently from theirs, it takes us a good deal of practice to be able to tell what horses are looking at.

EARS

How well can a horse hear? They can certainly hear higher notes than we can (at least up to 25 kcs and possibly more, whereas our limits are reached at about 20 kcs), though old horses, like old people, lose the higher end of the range. From their behaviour we know that horses can hear softer noises than we can: they will prick up their ears at the sound of approaching hoofs long before we can hear what they are listening to. This is partly due to the fact that they can move their funnel-shaped ears to collect sounds from particular directions. A horse has sixteen muscles to move his ear which gives him enormous accuracy in pointing. A horse that has heard something really interesting will swing his whole head, or even his body, round to bring both ears and both eyes into play as he examines it.

Ears also signal a horse's emotional state, and this use may interfere with hearing. A submissive dressage horse turns his ears back towards his rider, partly because his attention is on his rider but also because this ear position signals submission (*see page 72*); he cannot then hear what is going on ahead of him. An angry horse lays his ears flat back, and so can hear nothing at all.

SMELL

There has been no work done on the sensitivity of the horse's nose, so we have only behavioural evidence to go by. A free horse occasionally sniffs the wind, the better to identify a whiff of something that has caught his attention. Horses can certainly smell water from a good distance (mules are even better than horses) and the Mexican *vaqueros* say that a working cow-pony will smell a hidden cow from half a mile away. Horses also smell a trail when finding their way home, and mountain ponies sniff out the invisible sheep-tracks that lead safely across bogs. Choosing food is done mostly by smell: a horse offered unfamiliar food tilts her head first one way then the other as she examines it with each nostril in turn, and may then raise her head and roll back her upper lip in Flehmen as she uses her Jacobson's organ (*see overleaf*) to smell it more carefully.

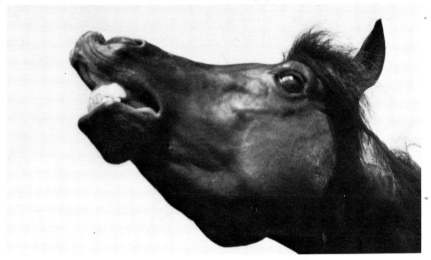

Plate 3 *Flehmen: Morgan stallion Shakertown smelling a mare's urine. After taking a deep whiff he raises his head, rolls his upper lip back and thus traps the smell-laden air in his Jacobson's organ. Flehmen (there is no English word for it) is also shown by other horses when they smell or taste something odd. Mares in pain when foaling also roll their upper lip back, though this seems to be a grimace of pain rather than an attempt to smell: they do show true Flehmen when licking the waters, the bag or the foal itself.*

Smelling other horses is particularly important, for to a horse each individual smells different. Mares identify their foals by smell, and two horses meeting put their noses so close together that they cannot see each other's ears and tail signals, and decide by smell alone whether to attack or to be friends. Horses also smell strange dung on a trail: stallions at least can tell the sex of the horse that dropped it, for they dung on another stallion's dung and urinate on a mare's. Horses smell our clothes with interest if we have been with other horses, and a stallion may become excited at the smell of an in-season mare on clothes. These identity-smells are *pheromones*, chemical messages that signal an animal's state. A person with a good sense of smell can tell the difference between a stallion's pheromones and those of a mare; in-season mares smell noticeably different again.

Jacobson's organ and Flehmen

Inside the horse's nose, at the back above the soft palate, there is a special pouch whose function, it has been suggested, may be to detect pheromones present in urine. The pouch, the Jacobson's or vomeronasal organ, is used when the horse does Flehmen: by inhaling deeply, then closing his nose by rolling up his upper lip, the horse can savour the smell better. But horses also show Flehmen when they taste something strange, so the organ is not used exclusively for urine analysis.

The Jacobson's organ is particularly well-developed in snakes (the flicking tongue of the snake picks up smell-laden particles and carries them to the organ for analysis) but other mammals, notably many hoofed mammals, cats, hyenas and bats, also have them as well as conventional smell-organs in the nose. All these animals show some kind of Flehmen: in a cat it is that open-mouthed, wrinkle-faced look that comes after smelling another cat's urine. Unable to close his nose by turning his lip over it, he does so by screwing his whole face up instead.

TASTE

We know little about a horse's sense of taste. Certainly they have a fine palate, as is shown by the way that they spit out food quickly if it tastes bitter. This sensitivity to bitterness is no doubt a help to their staying alive, since most poisonous plants are bitter. We can take our food in our hands, look at it and smell it before eating; a horse cannot, nor can he smell one tiny disagreeable plant in the midst of a clump of sweet-smelling grass, so he must rely heavily on his quick reaction to a taste. Horses naturally like sweet-tasting food and fruits.

TOUCH

The sense of touch varies over different parts of the body: the nose and muzzle have far more nerves coming from them than other parts of the body. This is because of the supply of nerves from the whiskers. Other well-supplied areas are the neck, withers, shoulders, coronet, and rear of the pastern. There are different types of touch-sensitive nerve endings, surface ones and deep ones (in addition to endings sensitive to heat and cold). These occur in different proportions over the body surface.

Table 1 *Discrimination*

Russian investigators using Pavlov's techniques of conditioned reflexes found that horses could tell the difference between:

1. Circles, triangles and squares drawn on cards.
2. Different colours, including red, violet and green.
3. A metronome ticking at 96 strokes per minute or at 100 strokes per minute.
4. Light intensity changes of 4 per cent (e.g., 96 watts and 100 watts).
5. Tones of 1000 cps and 1015 or 1025 cps (some of them found this difficult) i.e., between 1/4 and 1/7 of a tone.
6. A 500 cps tone at 69 Db and the same tone at 70 Db (Middle A on piano is 440 cps).
7. Similar loudness differences in a 1000 cps tone.

The pairs of stimuli were given randomly, one after the other (e.g. AABABBBAABAB) at intervals of a few minutes. This, say the investigators, shows sensitivity comparable to that of dogs. They do not mention what human sensitivity under similar conditions might be, but one suspects that the metronomes, the light intensities, and the loudnesses would be too difficult for us to tell apart. The reflex that was conditioned was leg withdrawal (*see also page 42*). (*Source: Popov, 1956*)

WHISKERS

The whiskers have a large and important nerve supply to the brain, but while they are known to be touch receptors we know little about their particular function in horses. They certainly tell the horse how far the end of his nose is from any surface: foals with their whiskers still crumpled tend to bump their noses on things, and horses wise to electric fences have been seen to test the current with their whiskers before touching the fence

with the rest of the body. Whiskers probably also give a horse a good deal
of information about textures, as when grazing, so they may be important
in feeding. Cutting a horse's whiskers off for cosmetic reasons means
depriving him of one of his vital senses: it is difficult to appreciate how
important whiskers may be since we do not have any, but that does not
mean they are dispensable. The same holds for the hairs inside a horse's
ears which protect his delicate eardrums from dust and invaders: to shave
them off is to ask for trouble.

Table 2 *The relative importance of different senses in mating stallions*

A number of stallions, both young (inexperienced) and old, were tested for their reactions
to an in-season mare or a dummy. The percentage that mated with the mare or dummy
was as follows:

Stallions	With mare	With dummy	With dummy sprinkled with mare's urine
young, normal	78	0	37
young, blindfold	85	9	
old, normal	100	79	
old, blindfold	100	38	

(*Source: Veeckman and Odberg, 1978*)

When 3 experienced stallions were given a cow to mate they reacted as follows according
to whether they were normal, blindfold, or masked so that they could not smell:

	Number of trials	Erection	Mounting
normal	4	0	0
blindfold	4	1	0
no smell	3	0	0
no smell, blindfold	7	7	5

(*Source: Estes, 1972*)

These experiments show: **(a)** the importance of experience: the old stallions mounted the
mares every time, though the younger ones did not. The experienced stallions would
mount a dummy fairly readily, probably because they came out expecting to mate. **(b)**
The main influence of sight and smell seems to be that if they are 'wrong' they stop
mounting behaviour. Stallions who could only feel, but not see or smell, would mount a
cow, and younger ones mounted both mares and dummies more readily if they could not
see: that is, if the stimulus was 'wrong' or frightening the stallions would not mount,
though in the absence of the wrong stimulus they would.

3
Mental Adaptation

Physically the horse is superbly adapted to life on an open plain or mountain. He copes well with other types of places too (for example, wet mountains as in Wales, woodland as in the New Forest, sandy coast as on Chincoteague and Assoteague, marshland as in the Camargue). But all the horse's physical adaptations would be useless if its behaviour were not adaptive too. A wild horse that showed no fear of wolves or swamps, or could not remember the way to water, would soon be dead; so would its bloodline if it could not manage to mate. Just as natural selection shapes bone, muscle, innards and skin to suit a particular way of life, it also shapes and refines the actions and reactions that make up an animal's behaviour so that mental adaptation is as finely tuned as physical adaptation. A horse does not, and cannot, think like a cat. Most horses, of course, do not live in the conditions to which they are so well-suited but in surroundings chosen by the whims of competitive cave-dwellers: small wonder that they sometimes behave as non-adaptively - stupidly, to our eyes - as fish flopping on a river bank.

What are the building blocks of behaviour, the psychic equivalent of tissues and organs, that evolution selects? What is the *psychological* 'ground plan' of a mammal's brain?

Unfortunately ethologists (who study animal behaviour) do not quite agree: there are several different schools of thought. All have evidence and argument to back them up, but their theories range from the extreme mechanistic approach of Skinner and the American behaviourists to the conceptual view of the Gestalt psychologists.

There is an old Sufi story about a group of blind men meeting an elephant for the first time. 'Ah,' says one, patting its side. 'It's like a wall.' 'No,' cries another, grasping its trunk. 'It's like a big snake.' 'You're both wrong,' yells the man who has bumped into its leg. 'It's like a treetrunk.'

'A flywhisk!' shouts the one with its tail. 'A sheet of leather,' says the one with its ears. And they all fall to fighting.

Different views of animal behaviour are a little like this. Some ethologists choose to watch deprived laboratory-bred rats pressing levers and others the behaviour of free-ranging wild gorillas. Frequently their views are not as contradictory as they first seem, though some are more limited than others. But the value of these years of patient experimenting and watching is that the scientific method sorts out which factors are relevant in certain conditions, however limited these might be, and the huge body of evidence that has gradually accumulated does show us the general principles on which animals' minds work. In attempting to get a clearer picture of horses than the blind men did of their elephant, we can call on first one school of thought and then another while remembering their limitations, and add this to the evidence of our own eyes.

Figure 11 *This rat in his 'Skinner box' has learned that if he presses the lever when the light is on he gets a food pellet as a reward. Using this technique scientists have found out a great deal about how animals learn: whether they work harder at a learned task when they are not rewarded every time; how they tell the difference between different signs flashed on the panel, and so on. In these unnatural conditions rats learn very slowly – they are also kept in boring cages that do not help to develop their minds – but the process is the same as in the rapid learning of their natural lives.*

Table 3 *Basic Code for Behaviour*

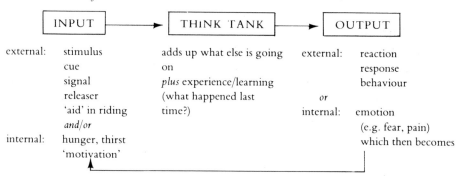

| INPUT | THINK TANK | OUTPUT |

external: | stimulus | adds up what else is going | external: | reaction
| cue | on | | response
| signal | *plus* experience/learning | | behaviour
| releaser | (what happened last | *or*
| 'aid' in riding | time?) | internal: | emotion
| *and/or* | | | (e.g. fear, pain)
internal: | hunger, thirst | | | which then becomes
| 'motivation' |

Reflexes are the simplest form.

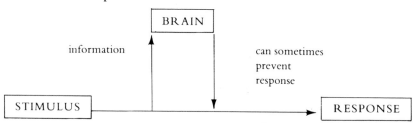

| BRAIN |

information | can sometimes
| prevent
| response

| STIMULUS | | RESPONSE |

Reflexes happen very fast and almost automatically, usually without any interference from the brain, for example:

knee tap ⟶ leg jerk
bright light ⟶ pupil closing (watch a cat)
in horses: light pressure on ⟶ skin twitch
hand flap near eye (e.g. fly) ⟶ blink

Although reflexes are mostly automatic, their strength may be changed by:

Inhibition: A deliberate order from the brain can stop the reflex from happening. (Stiffen your leg deliberately and it will not jerk when tapped.) But many reflexes, like the pupil-closing reflex, cannot be controlled easily.

Fatigue: Repeated hand flaps at a horse's head finally produce little or no response, though after a rest the blink comes back as strongly as ever. It is as if it simply got worn out for a while.

Many reflexes control walking and running: they make sure you do not use two opposite sets of muscles at the same time and jam yourself up. In horses, it is varied arrangements of these reflexes that produce the characteristic natural gaits – walk, trot, gallop – and it is not surprising that they are wired up differently to those in hopping animals like the kangaroo.

MODELS

Scientists studying natural processes often use models to mimic what they find and to explore their ideas. Sometimes these are actual models, like model aeroplanes in wind tunnels, but often they are just ideas, or strings of mathematical formulae. The first stage of investigation is to watch and observe; then, as patterns begin to emerge, a model is made. Finally, since the model-maker knows how his model will behave under certain conditions, he can test the animal, or system, in these conditions to see whether what the model predicts is true.

Often we find that one model works perfectly well up to a point, but that it is limited: we are only looking at the front end of the elephant. However, we can scrap the model, or modify it, until we come to one which seems to predict the system accurately. Good observations and results do not change, but they may be reinterpreted as evidence for a different theory.

At the moment the models of animal behaviour that seem most valuable come from the science of *systems analysis*. This tries to find out the rules of behaviour of any system – computers, economics, and animals too – by analysing the processes that are going on and the effects they have on each other. What rules does a computer follow when it is playing a game of chess? How does one economic trend affect another? What makes an animal eat when it does, and stop eating when it is full?

Systems analysis treats an animal as a design problem: how would we design an animal to do what it does? In order to do that we need to know first of all what it does, and how its behaviour satisfies its needs. And here we go straight back to the subject of adaptation, for it is immediately obvious that what it needs to do depends enormously on the type of life it follows. The animal's behaviour patterns are shaped by its evolution as much as is its body. Thus, the more we think of the horse's natural habitat, and the more we imagine how we would have to behave there, the better we understand his behaviour.

PROGRAMMES AND CHOICES

Having a well-designed body is no immediate recipe for survival: an animal needs to be able to look after that body, to search for goals like food, water, shelter and companions. J. Z. Young, the eminent neurobiologist, coined the term 'programs' for the different sequences of behaviour that lead the animal to these goals. Throughout its life the animal must choose between these programmes, summing up what is going on inside and outside itself and adding these to its experience before deciding what is the best programme to follow at the time, so that it is always behaving in an appropriate, adaptive way. If we think about what an animal needs to do to live, various programmes are obvious:

drinking;
eating;
looking after its coat or skin;
protecting itself from danger;
mating;
resting or sleeping.

Mammals, which suckle their young and produce small numbers of relatively helpless offspring, also have to:

nurse;
protect their babies.

Unless the animal is lucky enough to live constantly surrounded by food, drink, shelter and mates, it will have to:

know how to find the things it needs when the need arises, i.e. search, explore, remember.

Depending on the life the animal leads, it will also have its own particular programmes. A hunter has hunting programmes (search – stalk – kill – carry), a nest-maker ones for nest-making (find and recognize material – carry 'home' – arrange).

Many of these programmes come into action as a result of the animal's body states, though some, like the escaping or self-protecting ones, are responses to what is going on outside. The body state of dehydration makes the search for water increasingly important. When an animal has drunk enough to rehydrate itself it stops drinking and starts doing the next most important thing on its list, and so on. Sex hormones increase the importance of mating programmes; itches make grooming important; 'restlessness' makes movement or exploration the next thing to do. But what promotes 'restlessness'? We do not know exactly, and indeed the causes of some activities are much better understood than others although we do find that most of them follow the same general pattern.

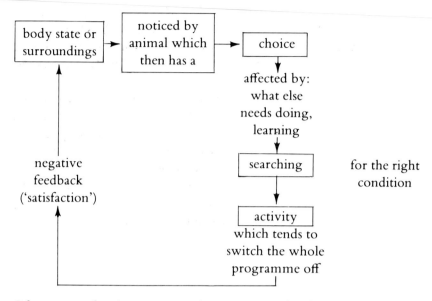

Of course, as the circumstances change so may the choices: an antelope at a waterhole will probably stop drinking and run away if a lion appears nearby. On the other hand, if the antelope is desperately thirsty and the lion appears to be thirsty rather than hungry, the antelope may decide to go on drinking while keeping a wary eye on the lion. Thus, some activities lose their importance when the need for others arises. In fact, not only do the activities lose their importance but the states that give rise to them do too. Anyone running for his life from a fire does not even feel hunger or pain, whatever he felt the moment before. Anyone who has been really hungry will know that feelings about itches, tiredness and even safety tend to disappear as the search for food becomes ever more important. The whole world starts to look rather different: our perceptions change.

Perception

The outside world presents an almost infinite variety of sights, smells, sounds, tastes and feelings, and it is impossible to absorb them all. These sensations are filtered out at three different levels, so that the animal tends to notice only what is useful to it at the time.

Firstly, the sense organs themselves only pick up certain sensations. As we have seen, horses' sense organs are quite different from ours, so that they do not hear or see the same things as we do. Although there are overlaps, our worlds are different. How fascinating it would be to trade sense organs with another animal, even for a brief half-hour!

Secondly, the areas of the brain that deal with sense information act as filters too in the way that they analyse that information. Thus though their eyes are not as sensitive as ours in most ways, horses are quicker to notice little fluttery movements than we are: these things are vitally important to their survival.

Thirdly, what the animal is thinking about acts as a filter even on that analysed information. A mating animal takes no notice of food; a frightened horse starts to notice only its escape routes. A hungry cat that is shown a mouse ceases to be able to hear a bell ringing: its brain literally switches its ears off. More usually this filtering is done at a higher level, so that the sensations still arrive at the brain but no notice is taken of them. This is what is loosely known as 'attention'.

All these filters are highly adaptive: that is, they work in such a way that the animal tends to know only about the things that are useful to it in its normal way of life.

Conflict

What happens when an animal has good reasons to do two incompatible things at the same time? It may be caught between the desire to approach something and the fear of doing so (approach/avoidance); or it may want to go two ways at once, as when frightened (avoidance/avoidance) or attracted (approach/approach) from two directions at the same time.

Unable to make up its mind, the animal tends to become agitated and bounce up and down on the only comfortable spot, or to run excitedly in circles round something it wants to approach and dare not. In the wild the last two types of conflict are usually fairly easily resolved: the animal runs off in a third direction, or goes towards whichever attraction it is facing. The donkey between its two piles of hay does not starve, but dithers about for a while until one pile is in front of it and it forgets about the other for the moment. Approach/avoidance conflicts may take a little longer to work out, and as the animal's conflict mounts it may well start behaving in a third, totally irrelevant way: it is as if it gives up the idea of approaching or going away and simply turns to the next thing on its list instead. Horses often snatch at grass when caught in this kind of conflict although eating is really far from their minds and is no solution: we see this often when, for instance, a stallion wants to approach a mare but dare not, or a horse is urged to cross a stream that frightens her. This type of behaviour (which was first described at a time when our theoretical interpretation of it was rather different) is called *displacement activity*. Displacement activities take their form in behaviour which usually occupies a fair amount of the animal's time anyway. Cats do a good deal of displacement grooming, while people often fiddle with their hands, and horses eat. Displacement eating is a nervous, hurried affair, noticeably unlike the placid munching of normal eating.

Other signs of conflict are agitated movements, some of which may take a stereotyped form, for example, headshaking in horses, nailbiting in people. Chronic conflict often results in nervous breakdown and neurosis (*see page 192*).

Frustration

When an animal is single-mindedly set on doing something and cannot because of the circumstances, it also becomes agitated and **FRUSTRATION OFTEN LEADS TO AGGRESSION.** How many of us have never attacked a machine in fury because it would not work, or got irritable because we needed sleep or food? Here we are behaving emotionally as an animal would. Indeed, some workers have felt that all aggression stems from frustration of one sort or another. This happens more often in abnormal conditions than in the wild, as when a hungry horse can see food going past her stable but cannot get at it. The more often this happens the more easily the connection is made, until the mere sight of food may trigger aggression.

Frustration can also lead to other forms of peculiar behaviour which depend rather on the individual's character. Chronically frustrated animals may also become miserable and listless, sinking into their own increasingly peculiar inner world: they 'pine', as may be seen in zoo animals. They may also develop tics and stereotypes, like stable vices, which represent an attempt to relieve themselves of the pressures within. Or they may go ahead and perform the behaviour they want to under conditions that are not the ideal ones but are fairly like them: thus in extreme hunger people will start eating things they do not normally classify as food, like sticks, rats, and even other people; barren mares with a strong maternal feeling may pinch other mares' foals; lonely animals (and people) may become attached to animals of other species and treat them like their normal herd-companions.

Fear and aggression

These states are often closely linked and in both cases the hormone adrenalin is produced, speeding up the heartbeat, increasing the blood sugar level and the flow of blood to the muscles in case they should have to work hard. It is adrenalin that makes us capable of that super-fast thinking and superhuman strength which surprise us in desperate circumstances.

Psychologically, too, fear and aggression are linked. Both are reactions to a state of affairs where things are not what the animal would want them to be. Although there are some states that always make an animal afraid and some that always make him angry, there is an area in the middle where how the animal reacts is greatly a question of his individual personality. Thus waving a stick at one horse may make him afraid, but it may enrage another horse and make him attack. We see this switch from fear to aggression when an animal cannot follow its fear programme and escape so it turns to attack instead, as in a frightened, cornered dog or horse.

While an animal must have self-defence programmes and spends a good deal of its young life perfecting them, there is no internal need for them to be performed: they are a reaction to conditions.

Maturation

Some behaviour programmes are only active at certain stages in the animal's life. The foal's 'mouthing' response which signals his submission to older horses disappears as the youngster nears sexual maturity; the suckling reflex becomes less important as time goes on and is replaced by a learned reaction that the mother finally discourages. In pigeons, flying is a behaviour pattern that develops with age. Although young pigeons seem to learn to fly over a period of a couple of weeks, it is not learning that is taking place but a slow turning on of the programme: pigeons prevented from practising flying during that time can, when released, fly just as well as those that have 'learned' to do so. That these programmes are turned on and off by the changes in hormonal levels associated with growing up seems likely: we know that sexual, mothering and nest-building behaviour in many animals varies according to the levels of sex hormones.

Critical periods

Some programmes have to be perfected by practice or learned within a certain period if they are to develop properly. In general, many of the social behaviour programmes of mammals have to be practised in youth or they do not develop fully, and the animal seems unable to learn them later in life.

Older ideas are mentioned briefly here because readers may be more familiar with them and wonder where they fit in.

What of 'instinct', a term so commonly used in talking about animal behaviour? There was a time when scientists split behaviour into two types, instinctive and learned, and this was based on the fact that many animals seem to know how to behave even though they may have had no opportunity to learn. Many seem to have a mental idea of a signal that they should respond to in certain ways, as if with a sequence of super-reflexes. Thus herring-gull chicks 'know' to peck at the orange spot at the end of the adult's bill, and the adult 'knows' in turn that when this happens it should regurgitate food for the chicks. Many animals with simpler brains, like insects and fish, behave in this way and are capable of very complicated, though rigid, 'instinctive' behaviour. But the division became more and more hazy when applied to the behaviour of mammals, which seemed to be able to learn to modify their 'instinctive' behaviour, and indeed clearly needed to practise a good deal of it. In short, the model became more and more limited, and because there had been so much argument about the term and what exactly it meant, it was dropped altogether.

However, that early work on instinct showed us things that, although we may interpret them differently now, are nevertheless true descriptions: the animals still do them. One idea was that of the specific releaser, like the spot on the herring-gull's bill, or the fuzzy picture that a foal has that makes him nuzzle for milk although he has never fed: this cue 'releases' a sequence of behaviour. These signals and patterns are usually called 'innate' now, meaning merely that the animal seems to be born with them without all the implications of the word 'instinct'.

'Drive' theory looked more closely at why an animal 'wants' to do something: to eat, to mate, to explore. It was thought that each of these different activities was governed by a drive from within the animal that demanded with increasing strength to be satisfied. But again this idea ran into difficulties when people tried to make drive the basis for all behaviour, and the models produced grew more and more complicated and controversial. Altogether it seemed better to try to look directly at the physical state of the animal that produces the 'need', and to consider the animal's choices and evolutionary history that govern its whole life pattern.

LEARNING

Learning is a change in response as a result of experience. There are different types:

1. *Habituation* is a temporary 'learning' not to respond to a certain cue, generally called 'getting used to it'. For example, after a series of loud bangs a horse stops startling so easily, though after a rest the response returns. After several habituation sessions the effect grows more permanent. How long it lasts depends on how thoroughly the habituation took place: as with all learning, timing is all-important.

Table 4 *Habituation of the mobbing response of chaffinches to a stuffed owl was studied. (When shown an owl, chaffinches shriek at it.)*

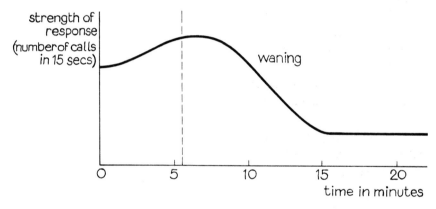

When the owl was removed, the response on next testing recovered, though not fully:

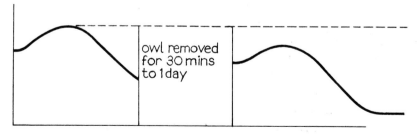

1. The most long-lasting effect was produced by repeated short exposures, not by a single long one.
2. In most habituation there is a *place effect*: habituation to a stimulus does not necessarily 'carry over' to the same stimulus in a different place.

Most early training in horses involves habituation: they get used to being caught, led and saddled in easy stages – and often they 'forget' their training in new places.

2. *Conditioned response* (also called Pavlovian, classical, operant or Type 1 learning) The animal learns to connect a new signal with one of its normal actions. Pavlov taught dogs that the sound of a bell meant that food was coming, so that after a while their mouths watered when the bell was rung; stud stallions learn, only too readily, that a particular halter means they are about to be used for mating, and grow sexually excited at the sight of it. Again, timing is all-important; the signal must come just before, or at the beginning of, the response, not after it. Repetition helps 'cement' the learning. *Rewards* are not as important in this type of learning as was once thought: often simple time-association is enough. Thus, we can teach a horse to trot on a lunge rein by merely saying 'trot' every time he happens to be about to do so; after a while the word produces the action.

Guthrie and the 'contiguity' theorists felt that *timing* and *repetition*, rather than reward and punishment, were the keys to learning. 'A combination of stimuli which has accompanied a movement will on its recurrence tend to be followed by that movement,' he stated. In other words, if in a given situation you do something, the next time the situation occurs you are likely to do it again – and the more often you have done it, the more likely you are to do it again. Thus *habit strength* is important in determining behaviour. Guthrie's ideas arose from practical observations of animals in their everyday lives, rather than an attempt to form an overall theory, and they are useful in practical training, particularly where the breaking of bad habits is concerned (*see page 181*).

3. *Trial-and-error learning* (Skinnerian, instrumental or Type II learning) The animal learns to make a new response in order to get a reward or avoid punishment after a certain signal. Skinner put rats or pigeons in 'Skinner boxes' where they found that pressing a lever brought a pellet of food. They could then be taught to press the lever only when a light was on, or to press it when a buzzer sounded to avoid an electric shock, and so on. Skinner, Watson and the American 'behaviourist' school hold that almost all behaviour can be explained from this mechanical reward/punishment scheme, and that an animal is little more than a collection of such associations: there is no need for ideas such as programmes or understanding. His novel *Walden Two* describes a futuristic human society based entirely on this scheme. Though his ideas work well in laboratory condi-

tions, they cannot explain many of the effects seen in 'real life', like latent learning and insight.

Shaping is the term Skinner coined for the way that a new response is gradually built up by rewarding only increasingly accurate responses. For example, in training circus animals the trainer at first rewards just a movement in the right direction, then a step or two, then a whole action, until he has 'shaped' a complete new trick. Shaping takes a part in our teaching the more advanced movements on cue to a horse: at first we praise any effort in the right direction, but only later reward a perfect response.

4. *Latent learning* is 'hidden' learning done without any immediate reward, e.g. forming mental maps of an area during explorations. Horses are particularly good at this, and if left to their own devices show clearly how well they understand the geography and interests in the area they have been ridden over; if you think you can probably remember where you last saw, say, a pair of yellow gloves although at the time you noticed them you had no good reason for remembering the fact.

5. *Insight learning* is the sudden realization of the solution to a problem without trial and error. A dog separated from food by a fence twenty feet long soon realizes that he can run round the end of the fence. Most horses do not: if they do learn to make the detour it is generally because they have become so excited they are galloping around and happen to come to the end of the fence. In fact horses are not good at insight, probably because in the wild there is no particular reason for them to be; we, problem-solvers by nature, are superbly good at it and tend to think that any animal that is not is profoundly stupid.

Bright young horses in training sometimes show insight on being given new cues for the first time, for example, on being asked to rein back. When the rider gives the 'go' signal the horse prepares to move forward, meets with resistance from the hands and, if he is calm, adds two and two together and concludes that the only way to go is backwards.

6. *Imprinting* is a special form of learning that is especially striking in birds but also occurs in mammals. How does a horse know that he is a horse, not a cow, a person or a goat? Simply, a foal is born with an innate desire to follow anything that moves, especially anything large. After a few days he grows choosy and only follows the one that has given any satisfaction so far – normally his mother. This 'imprints' the image of his species-identity, and later he socializes and mates with animals like that image. Isolated

orphan foals often imprint on humans so that they literally think they are people: this can have dire consequences when they grow big, sexy, playful and pushy. Konrad Lorenz's *King Solomon's Ring* describes imprinting in domestic birds (and other forms of behaviour too) most delightfully. Imprinting may be the reason behind the colour-preference shown by some stallions: it may be that they only want to mate with mares the same colour as their mothers (*see page 96*).

LEARNING involves:

(a) *Timing*. The stimulus and the response must occur together *or within a second* or the connection between the two is not made.

(b) *Repetition* helps strengthen the connection although one-trial learning does occur. (Horses, particularly Arabs, remember spots where something frightened them and may take a long time to 'forget' the unpleasantness.) Generally, the more natural survival value there is in learning the faster it happens. Guthrie held that repetition is highly important: *in any situation the animal tends to do what it did last time, and only a change of circumstances produces a different response.*

(c) *Reinforcement*, both positive (reward) and negative (aversion and punishment) strengthen the connection, too. Rewards work much better than punishment, and they work better if they are not given every time but rather less often as training progresses. Punishment works only when it stops the response so that no repetition takes place; it is particularly useless if applied after the complete response. In animals that are especially prone to fear, like horses, punishment tends to arouse such strong feelings and escape reactions that it prevents any possibility of learning, especially learning new responses.

(d) *Stimulus generalization/discrimination*

Where is the dividing line between black and white? If you had learned that black was 'good' (brought food) and white 'bad' (brought punishment) how would you respond to the greys? It would probably depend on how hungry you were and how afraid you were of punishment – in other words, on the strength of the feelings involved. On the whole, the stronger the feeling the more you would 'generalize' in its favour. If you knew that black brought only a peanut but white meant a fearful beating you would probably take no chances and call all the greys white. But if you were starving and knew that black brought a good meal and white only a mild rebuke you would probably risk calling all the greys black. Generally, the grey areas bring confusion in learning. It is true of most mammals that too much of this confusion results in hypertension, irritability and finally breakdown and neurosis. Pavlov taught dogs that responding to a circle brought food but responding to an oval brought an electric shock. When he gradually rounded the oval he found that about half of them had complete nervous breakdowns (*see page 192*). Horses that have been trained by novices who are inconsistent in presenting cues often become extremely upset.

(e) *Forgetting* (extinction of the response) happens when the connection is not re-used, but the rate at which it happens depends on how thorough the learning was in the first place.

Gestalt psychologists stressed that an animal does not respond simply to a cue but to a set of conditions of which the cue is only one. 'The whole,' they said, 'is more than a sum of its parts.' Unlike the American behaviourists, they emphasized the importance of the animal's perception and understanding of the whole situation, or Gestalt. Their attitude is helpful in understanding latent learning and insight learning (which is seen as a mental rearrangement of the animal's idea of the Gestalt). When we fail to recognize a familiar face in an unfamiliar setting it is because the Gestalt, the whole, has changed; when a horse is alarmed at a new arrangement of familiar objects (like barrels lying about the field) it is because the Gestalt is unfamiliar; and when a horse that has been trained to respond a certain way at home fails to do so in a new place it is again because the Gestalt has changed. Training a horse so that his whole attention is on us is to become his Gestalt.

Programmes for learning

Evolution, through selection, has built the biological base so that many behaviours are easily, almost inevitably, learned.

(S. L. Washburn, a leading authority on primate behaviour)

They forget that even the capacity to learn, to learn at all, to learn only at a definite stage of development, to learn one kind of thing rather than another, to learn more or less quickly, must have some genetic basis.

(Julian Huxley, of the American behaviourists)

Learning is not like writing new information on a blank sheet of paper: even learning has its programmes. Different kinds of animals learn different kinds of things more or less easily. This is partly because of physical ability (it is no good trying to teach a dog to read small print, for apart from anything else it cannot see well enough). But it also depends on what kinds of things are useful for the animal to learn in its natural surroundings – that is, on their survival value.

Horses are particularly good at learning:

places where something special happens;

paths, directions, mental maps;

sounds (since they 'talk' to each other they understand that different sounds have different meanings);

who is who;

what smells taste like (in recognizing grasses and shrubs);

particular movements;

what is not dangerous (since they are so defenceless they tend to think everything dangerous until proved safe, i.e., the innate reaction is easily modified by learning).

DEVELOPMENT OF A PROGRAMME

In the chain of events that form a programme learned and innate responses interact. Young animals seem to be born with a number of innate instructions, like *follow anything big that moves*, or, *move towards a nicker*, which leads them into a number of scrapes from which they learn. For instance, the suckling behaviour of a new-born foal is a complicated thing to arrange, if we imagine trying to tell him what to do. How should he know where to go? 'Mother' is meaningless to a thing half-an-hour old. What is he looking for, since he has never tasted food? In fact he only has to have one innate instruction: *push in the shadow between two large uprights*.

Thus finding a dark cavern between two uprights, the foal sticks his head in. Possibly he finds a place between two trees, or between the gatepost and the fence, in which case he will persist until something else stops him; possibly he gets between the mother's front legs, in which case she redirects him. But if he is in the right place, his nosing about hits a teat bursting with . . . milk. He gets a drop on his nose; he licks it off; his licking stimulates the mother's let-down reaction: more milk flows. Sooner or

Figure 12 *This tiny foal, straying from his mother, is attempting to suckle from a deep crack in the bark of the tree because it appears to offer him the 'right' signs for suckling: a dark crack between two uprights. His mother is calling him back.*

later he gets the teat in his mouth, and instantly his *strong suckling reflex* comes into play (foals will suck anything). Big rewards follow. This has two consequences: first, he will tend to repeat what he has just done, which means that his attachment to his mother gets stronger and he imprints on her; second, he will tend to repeat it in wrong places too. Either he gets no reward, and gives up, or, if he tries it on other horses, they will drive him away crossly. Increasingly he learns that there is only one place that really works. From one simple innate instruction, and one reflex, this complicated behaviour is built up and perfected until all the chancey elements have disappeared. (It is a happy circumstance that when we first bottle-feed foals we usually hold the bottle in a 'right' place; if not, it can be very difficult to persuade a foal to look somewhere else.)

Discovered patterns

Some behaviour patterns are 'discovered' by almost all horses simply because of their physical shape, for example, scratching behind the ear with the back foot; how to lie down (not many positions are comfortable); how to roll successfully (foals spend a lot of time sleeping flat, and they discover little by little how to scratch their necks and their backs while lying down). Some of these patterns may be copied from other horses, and some horses miss out on the discoveries; but they may find other ones instead, like how to scratch behind their ears on convenient people.

Adaptabrain

The brain has often been compared to a miraculous kind of living computer, its input being the various sensations and feelings coming both from the outside world and from the animal's body, its output being behaviour, with programmes that link the two. What kind of programmes might we expect our plains-dwelling browser/grazer to have? What programmes would be most useful for it? It would not survive long if it had the same programmes as a cat, for instance: its innate reactions would be out of

Plate 4 *George Stubbs'* Horse attacked by a lion *shows only too vividly how helpless a horse is if he has not run away quickly enough. Even horses that have been raised in safe lion-free conditions are constantly aware of the possibility of this horror, and take care it should not happen to them. For us, remembering about these imaginary lurking lions and sabre-tooth tigers is a short cut to understanding the basic mentality of the horse.* (Photo: Courtesy of the Tate Gallery, London)

place, and it would not be programmed to learn better ones. So what should a horse be equipped with?

Apart from the usual problems of breathing, eating, drinking and keeping itself in good trim, the first, major and vital problem of being a horse is that it is **ALMOST TOTALLY DEFENCELESS AND IT TASTES GOOD.** Its teeth can bruise but not tear; a well-aimed kick might knock out a lion but a horse cannot see where to aim well. Its best defence is escape, and it must always be alert to the need for escape. 'Wild horses and other hoofed mammals can only run away. This characteristic feature is the focal point, so to speak, on which all the other psychic and somatic properties of the horse depend.' (Hediger, 1955) *Running away*, then, is a powerful natural reaction (*see page 85*).

Alertness to danger is another necessity, and here the problem deepens. A grass-eater has to spend a good deal of its time eating, especially in the winter. Then how can it spend enough of its time eating but remain alert enough not to get eaten?

The solution, which is the one that has evolved in almost all big herbivores, is to live in a group or herd. In a herd, animals can take turns watching while others eat or rest: many pairs of eyes and ears are better than one. But for the animals in a herd to stay together they must want to do so. In other words, there will be strong social feelings.

This has far-reaching consequences. It means there must be some way of organizing the herd into a unit; that there must be some means of communication between the members of the herd; that the ways of choosing a mate will follow certain patterns.

> The ox . . . cannot endure even a momentary severance from his herd. If he be separated from it by stratagem or force, he exhibits every sign of mental agony; he strives with all his might to get back again, and when he succeeds he plunges into its middle to bathe his whole body with the comfort of close companionship.
>
> (Francis Galton, of South African cattle, 1871)

4

Social Life

LIVING IN A GROUP

No horse likes to live alone, and few do it by choice. Many horses are forced to get used to solitude, but wild or free-ranging horses seldom live alone. Even domestic horses who have never known real danger feel more comfortable in company: horses are social animals.

We, too, are social animals and have the same innate desire for company, although some of us may have learned to like solitude or even to fear other people. But almost all of us know what loneliness and isolation bring: fear, nervousness, restlessness, a yearning for someone we feel relaxed with, and finally simple misery. Where we reach for the telephone, listen with fading hope to unanswered ringing, and get up to light a cigarette or fiddle with something, the horse calls out, listening with tremendous concentration for the reply and, when there is none, stamps restlessly round his stall. Displacement activities take over: many lone horses, especially in new and frightening surroundings, cannot keep still and only snatch at their food. Company, even human company (stimulus generalization), soon settles and reassures them.

Stallions, because of their 'possessiveness', have an even greater need for company than other horses (*see page 138*) and some become wildly miserable, and even vicious, if kept alone. A goat, donkey, sheep or even a goose will, at a pinch, satisfy their desperate need for company and reduce the hypertension so common in solitary confinement. Pets do the same for lonely people.

Horse groups

Wild horses kill two birds with one stone: they combine the need for company with the need for finding a mate, so that most natural groups are *breeding units*. Mostly these consist of:

one stallion;

a few mares (2–20, usually 4 or 5);

their foals;

their yearlings;

one or two 2-year-olds.

Total: around a dozen, more with a strong stallion, fewer with a less successful one.

Obviously there are some stallions, usually the young, timid or old ones, which do not have any mares. They do not usually live by themselves but in bachelor groups. Pelligrini, who studied wild horses in Montana, found one old, mareless stallion which had teamed up with an elderly buck antelope rather than roam alone: old stallions who have lost their harems to younger, stronger studs find it difficult to tolerate the presence of other males and may wander alone until they accept being part of a bachelor group. Strong young colts, which are driven out of the parent band by the stallion as they reach maturity, often pair to go on marauding expeditions in search of straying mares; they are more likely to pinch a stallion's mare when his back is turned than to challenge him directly. In one Canadian study of mustangs, sixteen out of the twenty-two horses that changed bands were yearlings or two-year-olds; the others may have been young too but this is difficult to tell in long-range observations of wild horses.

The composition and size of wild horse bands varies a good deal according to the circumstances, so that although their feeling for social life is strong horses have few preconceived ideas about how it should be arranged. Domestic horses running together in large areas also split themselves up into bands even when no stallion is present, but the study of ponies running loose in the New Forest showed that when there are too few stallions the groups may be smaller and are usually based on families, or the families of mares that are friends. There are also more single mares. Presumably, then, it is mostly the stallion's herding behaviour that keeps the harems together and stable.

WHO'S WHO IN THE GROUP

The popular view of wild horse bands is that they roam around headed by a proud stallion who nobly protects them from all dangers and fights off intruders. Unfortunately the facts do not fit this romantic picture. Later misconceptions include the view that horses organize themselves on the basis of a 'peck order' (*see page 55*) but on closer examination this does

Table 5 *Studies on wild horse populations*

Results of such studies show that horse groups vary in size and behaviour according to
the type of land they are on.

	Pryor Mts (Montana) open mountain, fairly dry	Grand Canyon (Arizona) steep, desert	Sable Island (East coast, US) sandy, flat	Shackleford Bank (East coast, US) sandy and marshy
Total number	225	78	240	104
Density per sq. km	2	0.2	6.3	11
Age structure:				
adults	58%	?	64%	61%
youngsters	28%		21%	21%
foals	13%		15%	19%
Group range	25 sq. km	20 sq. km	under 7 sq. km	6 sq. km
Defended territories	no	no	no	yes: 3 sq. km
Average adults in				
group: harems	5.0	4.5	6.0	12.3
bachelor groups	1.8	?	2.0	2.6
solitary males	few	few	few	few
temporary banding				
into big herds	no	no	yes	yes
band stability:				
mare changes per				
year	7.6%	none	?	10.8%
Source:	(Feist)	(Berger)	(Welsh)	(Rubenstein)

In the dry, open mountains (Marlboro country) small bands of horses have huge, overlapping ranges and a few mares drift from group to group; in this harsh country infant and
old-age mortality is high. In the vertical desert of the Grand Canyon the ranges do not
overlap so much and the bands remain separate, each probably in its own side-canyon. But
on the wetter islands the ranges are much smaller (more food and water). On the relatively
lush Shackleford Bank the population is so high that on one end of the island the stallions,
with large harems, defend their territories - not entirely successfully, since their mares do
stray.

On the East Coast islands, as in the marshy Camargue (Southern France), bands may
group together in large herds when loafing (up to 80 in the Camargue) especially in
summer. Camargue horses have been shown to get bitten by horseflies less often when
they are in large groups than when they are in small groups. The fact that horses group in
marshy places in the summer but not in the winter nor in dry country suggests that they do
it as a protection against bloodsucking flies. Although most adult stallions will not let other
adult stallions near their mares (and they tend to feel more strongly about this in the
summer than in the winter) they will tolerate such closeness if it means suffering less misery
from flies.

not prove true either. Then how do horses organize their social life? The view that is generally emerging is that, although the ways that horses feel about each other follow a consistent pattern, their differing circumstances mean that their lives are played out in different ways, so that at first sight quite contrasting and misleading pictures may emerge.

However, the common thread running through all horse societies seems to be that families are important, and so is friendship. To start with the simplest group, the stallionless families found, for example, in the New Forest: youngsters even after they are weaned tend to stay with or around their mothers, and although they grow more independent and exploratory as they grow older, they still tend to follow the mother if she makes off in a determined fashion. In a small family group, then, the mother is usually the leader when they are on the move, and she is usually the first to drink, to roll, and so on.

Friendship is also a strong and important link. Friendship in domestic horses is only too well known: pairs of friends loaf about together, swishing flies off each other's faces; they scratch each other's withers; they like to travel together when out in a group; and they get wildly miserable when they are parted. The reasons why they get such strong feelings about each other may be a little baffling but sometimes we can see what they are. Sometimes friends have simply been together for a long time; sometimes they have been thrown together at a time when life in general was a little threatening, as when first weaned, or by chance introduced together into an already existing group. But whatever the reasons, wild horses show the same kinds of feelings about each other. In a group grazing freely, or loafing, or dozing, we tend to find the same horses close together, and it is the ones that they stay closest to that they groom most often.

In any pair of friends one is likely to be bolder, or less nervous, than the other, and so may be the leader not only of her family but also of her friend and her friend's family, for each of them has reasons to follow another. In these double-family groups, then, we might see leadership as important although in a way it is the links that cause 'follower-ship' that are keeping the horses in their places.

In the larger harem, the stallion's job is not to be the leader but the herdsman. It is his herding behaviour (*see page 79*) that keeps the group together, so that far from being the leader he is usually the follower, threatening the heels of the stragglers. In some cases he may look like the leader, as when he goes ahead to challenge another stallion, or when he overtakes the harem to be the first to drink at a waterhole, which seems to be usual behaviour in the mustang groups.

Plate 5 *Group of free-living Navajo ponies on the move. Although the Navajo use*
these horses, they are left to roam free and make their own social arrangements like truly
wild horses. They are making off after I disturbed them. The leader mare concentrates on
the path ahead; her friend, the second adult mare, keeps close to her. Third in line is the
leader mare's daughter; then comes the white stallion, taking a typical herding position
near the back, between his mares and the danger. The youngest mare in the harem, the
white-faced mare's daughter, has just pulled back a bit: a moment before, the stallion had
herded her too near the heels of the leader mare's daughter (note her ears). Only the
leader mare wears a headcollar, for the links of the group mean that if she is caught so are
all the others. Applying practical psychology means that when travelling, camping or
picnicking you usually need only tether one horse if it is the right one. Having a stallion
along to keep the others herded helps too. Like other Indians (and gypsies) the Navajo
like 'coloured' horses in their mustang-bred stock. Vermillion Cliffs, Arizona, just east
of the Grand Canyon.

Since the stallion collects mares he may well collect ones that do not feel
particularly friendly towards each other, and some that may be unfriendly
all round, and this is reflected in the way that these mares do not choose to
spend time together but are always found at opposite ends of the group. In
these larger groups there is a complicated network of bonds that link
certain horses together, and a lack of them that keeps others apart so that
there are only certain patterns that all of them feel comfortable with.
When they are following each other in a line there are probably not many

solutions to this complicated equation, so that they may well follow each other in the same order of march and in doing many other activities.

The family and friendship links are constantly shown in many forms of closeness, in grooming, loafing, dozing and playing together. Mares do not allow other mares' foals to suckle them, and usually drive them away but the stallion plays with any foals, even young colts, so that all the youngsters know him well. He usually has favourite mares that he likes to be with and to groom even when they are not in season: friendship is important to him too. However, it is he who drives the mature colts out of the band.

Stallions in bachelor groups stay together because of friendship and dislike of solitude. Here again there may be a habitual leader and habitual followers.

The feelings that dictate the structure of the band, then, are: family links; friendship; and pressure from the stallion.

'PECK ORDERS' AND 'DOMINANCE'

Anyone who knows a group of horses kept together in a field will know that there is often one of them that bosses the others around. He, or she, is the first at the gate for handouts, the one in the shade when there is not enough for all, the one to drive the others away from their food with threats and bites. Similarly there is often one poor harassed creature that seems to get knocked about by all the others, and spends his mealtimes in a state of almost constant nervousness lest one of the others decides to come and bully him.

Early research on farmyard hens had shown that they could be ranked in a 'peck order' such that A, the bossiest, pecked all the others; B, the second, pecked all but A, and so on down the line. The aggressive hens high in the peck order, the 'dominant' ones, are the first at the food trough, while the 'submissive' ones that give way to all the others have to hang back. It was thought that the peck order or dominance hierarchy was the main basis for the way that many animal groups organized themselves, especially when it was seen that the peck order seldom changes.

People working with horses saw evidence of this type of peck order in horses, and thought that the aggressive, or 'dominant' horses, which are often the biggest, strongest (and best fed) of the group, were the leaders seen in wild horse groups. However, this is not true. More detailed and careful studies, many on the famous Tour du Valat herd of Camargue

ponies whose breeding and relationships have been studied for years, have
shown that the bullies are not necessarily the leaders, and that the strongly
developed 'peck orders' we see in domestic horses are mostly the result of
their being kept in conditions where competition matters and of studying
them during those competitions. In their natural state horses do not have
small piles of food to argue over; they do not have to jostle for attention
and titbits and space through gateways; and although it is true that some
of them are more aggressive than others, and resent others coming near
them, that does not have anything to do with how they organize their
groups – or, indeed, any other characteristics of their behaviour. Scientists,
mostly in the US, who still believe in the importance of peck orders, have
tested to see whether aggressiveness has any bearing on learning ability or
trainability and have found that it has not; and indeed a moment's thought
will show that there is no particular reason why a horse that is bad-
tempered towards other horses should be any brighter or more intelligent
than any other. Moreover, we can see that aggressive horses are likely to
go on being aggressive so that the peck order will be stable. It has,
incidentally, been found that aggressive mares tend to produce aggressive
foals.

Dominance hierarchies, then, turn out to be a result of conditions and
of a point of view: as far as being clues to what governs horse society they
are a red herring. But that does not mean that they do not exist at all, and
where they do exist they may be important in management.

Where competition has produced a 'peck order' in a group of horses,
the group will tend to bully a newcomer into being submissive, so that
care should be taken about introducing a new horse into the group: it is a
good idea to put him into the next field first for a few days so that he can
be befriended without being bullied. Where one horse is being bullied by
all the others we cannot persuade the others to 'be nice' to him: we have
to change the feeding arrangements or the group. Youngsters are submissive to threats from older horses, so a single youngster in a group of adults
is unlikely to do well. Submissive horses do not like going near the bullies,
so when a horse refuses to pass or to go near another, it is worth wondering
whether bullying has anything to do with the refusal (there may, of course,
be other reasons) and whether he has spotted the slight hint of a threat that
we may well not have noticed.

Before the idea of dominance hierarchies collapsed entirely, scientists
looking at other animal societies started to see that aggression is not the
only key to dominance. M. R. A. Chance, a leading authority on primate
groups, said: 'Broadly speaking, dominance is at present considered to be

Plate 6 *Stallionless band of horses on a stud farm in Tasmania. Coming up the rise, the front horses stop in surprise at seeing a camera. The front two (centre) are friends, as are the two on the right: note how close both pairs are standing. The others have been slopping along more or less in line behind the leaders, except for an independent youngster (left) who is exploring a line of his own. This looks to be perfect horse country.* (Photo: Louise Serpa)

that attribute of an animal's behaviour which enables it to attain an object
when in competition with others . . . . A more rewarding way of defining
the dominance status of a supremely dominant animal is that he or she is
the *focus of attention* of those holding subordinate status within the same
group.' Attention studies have not been done on horses, but it is interesting
to note that insistence on attention encourages submissiveness in them too
(*see page 168*).

Natural understanding of friendship, need for social contact, and willingness
to follow shapes the whole attitude of social animals. It is no coincidence
that all the animals we find easy to train are ones that live in groups and
have this natural understanding of friendship and contact. Horses, dogs,
elephants, oxen, seals and dolphins are all social animals. Cats and tigers
are not, and while there is nothing lacking in their intelligence (they are
quick to learn for a food reward) we find that they will not work for us
with the same willingness as social animals. 'It is no accident that dogs
certainly have an inherited capacity to show recognition that they have
done wrong, but cats never show guilt,' writes J. Z. Young. Unlike dogs
and horses, cats do not particularly care what we think of them.

   Just as horses have different relationships with each other, they have
different ones with us too. Rough breaking methods rely heavily on the
aggressive side of dominance; this produces fear which, although allowing
habituation, tends to confuse and prevent higher forms of learning. While
placid horses submit, others try vigorously to escape whenever possible;
the naturally aggressive ones often refuse to submit and start fighting back
while some, like the harassed members of a group, quietly wait their
chance to get their own back.

   More successful methods of advanced training rely on the 'focus of
attention' idea to achieve submission, using relatively boring and familiar
surroundings to help ensure that the horse's attention does not wander
from his rider. Once trained, such horses are completely reliable in the
show ring or dressage arena, for they notice nothing but their rider's cues;
on the other hand they may be hopelessly anxious in circumstances where

*Plates 7 and 8 Once they have learned not to fear people, horses tend naturally to
generalize their social feelings and extend them to us: we become, as it were, honorary
horses. If you scratch a horse's back he will scratch yours, as if you were a horse; if you
offer friendship to a lonely horse he will treat you as a friend; and if you show the same
qualities of boldness and good judgement as a natural leader, he will follow you through
thick and thin.*

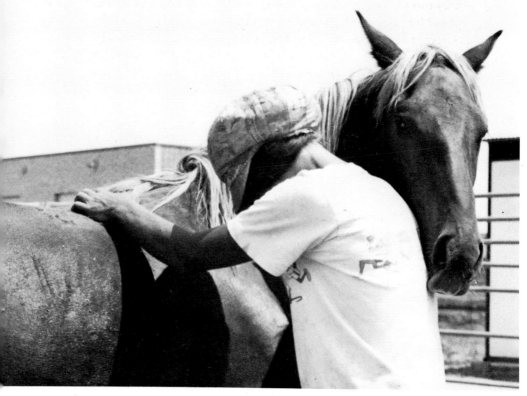

the rider's attention is distracted from them or where they have to think for themselves, and dangerous when they escape.

Different schools of advanced training demand different degrees of submission, following, or freedom of thought from the horse. Often a whole system of training is built on a required attitude, so that advice on handling problems can be confusing sometimes if taken out of context. Thus, for instance, a horse which responds because of bonds of friendship will get thoroughly upset when heavy-handed dominance ideas are applied to him, while a horse that has always been treated in a domineering fashion may at first take advantage of kinder attitudes.

Plate 9 *There are many horses, especially pleasure horses and ponies, that have established a relationship of friendship and trust with their riders rather than one of dominance and submission. While not particularly obedient in the show ring, these ponies come to be safe, tolerant and willing, as friendly and communicative to their owners as they would be to a paddock companion, and confidently wise about the world. Leading rein class, Highland show.* (Photo: Louise Serpa)

5

Communication

Social life depends on communication, on sending and receiving signals that other members of the group understand. While some appear to be deliberately sent as messages – threat faces, some calls, human speech – others, like body postures, seem to be almost involuntary expressions of the animal's inner state which, however, can be understood by onlookers.

Calls, positions, movements and chemical messages are the ways in which an animal expresses itself.

CALLS

Horses make several different calls.

The neigh is a contact/recognition call: 'Where are you?' 'Anybody there?' or 'Hi!', rather like our initial 'Hello?' on the telephone. As there are great differences in individual voices, horses can recognize their companions by their neighs, which are thus important in keeping groups together: a separated member neighs hopefully and can tell from the reply whether it comes from one of her group or from a stranger. The mere sound of a familiar neigh can set off a long exchange in separated friends. Isolated horses tested with recordings of neighs reply more to those of their herd-companions than to those of others; mares recognize recordings of their foals' neighs, although foals do not appear to be able to recognize their mothers' voices individually (*Gann 1981*). A stallion's neigh is recognizable by the extra grunt given at the end, and to a certain extent we can also learn to tell the difference between breeds from their neighs: our Welsh mountain ponies characteristically have clear, ringing, musical neighs, while the Welsh cobs' neighs are usually shorter, hoarser and less melodic.

Neighs have been completely misunderstood by Hollywood film-makers who constantly re-run that same potted neigh in fear/alarm situations

Plate 10 *Challenging neigh of an adult stallion, Flying W Little Thunder, whose small size does not deter him from feeling full of himself. Full of attention to the scene, he raises his head to allow his throat room for expansion, as we do when we are trying to sing high notes. Thunder is a full-grown miniature.*

where horses would not neigh; but in the 'creeping-up-on-the-enemy-camp' scenes their tethered horses do not neigh at the sound and smell of approaching horses, whereas real ones would.

Nickers are shorter and lower, and used at closer range: 'come closer, friend'. They fall into three groups:

1. The type given to friends as a greeting and 'come' signal when friends are near enough to be recognized. Human friends bringing food are often called with nickers.
2. The stallion courtship nicker, low, long and forceful, given by a stallion to a mare he wishes to mate.
3. The soft maternal nicker of a mare calling her foal to her side. Young foals' response to this appears to be innate: as soon as they are born they come to an imitated nicker. Again they do not recognize their mothers' voices individually, but simply run to the sound at first; later they become more selective.

Sonagrams are pictures of sounds reproduced like a graph. The higher the note, the higher it is on the scale: on this scale 2½ is middle C, and 5 the C an octave above. The louder the note is, the darker the mark.

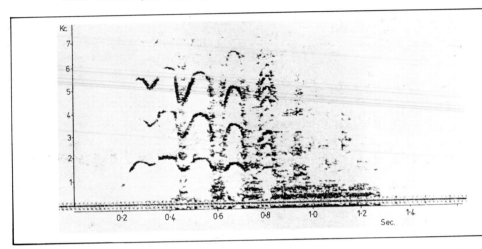

1. The musical neigh of a mare. Here we can see three clear notes, or harmonics, which go up and down in little bursts.

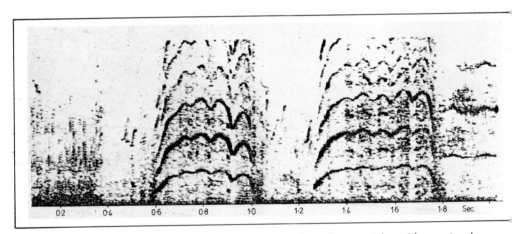

2. A stallion's short neighs to an in-season mare. Here there are at least 6 harmonics, the main one centring around middle C and the others going off the scale of the instrument. The notes start and end low, but do not go up and down as much as the mare's: the stallion is excited and is doing a flat, bellowing type of neigh although it is still a musical one.

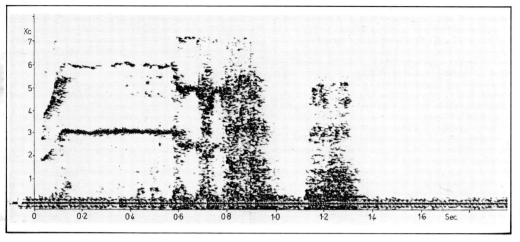

3. The shrieking neigh of a small foal taken away from his mother. He holds one note steady and ends up with an unmusical snort. Here there is only one harmonic so that he is making a thin sound unlike the rich chord of the stallion's call.

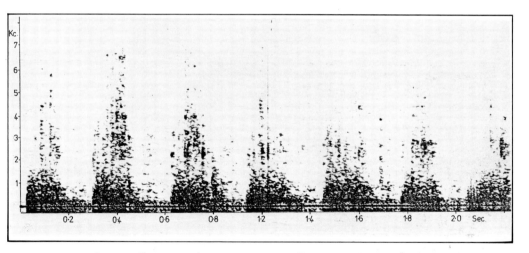

4. Snorts from a stallion. Here there are no notes at all, just quick bursts of noise which begin and end abruptly.

The three neighs are quite different, partly because they came from different animals but also because the animals were in different states of mind. A panicky neigh, like this foal's, is flatter and less melodic than the ordinary call. The wide variation in the way that calls are given means that there is often no clear distinction between one call and another, so that different observers may classify them a little differently. (Sonagrams: Sheila Gann)

Squeals are used in very close contact, especially sexual. Flirty mares squeal during courtship and also when meeting strangers. Often this goes with a stamp of the forefoot. These squeals are signs of excitement and arouse the other horse at the same time as warning him to take care and not be too familiar, so they show resentment too. (Indignant, warning squeals are used in kicking matches and fights, and in bucking bouts when the bucks are seriously meant.)

Snorts in wild horses are alarm and challenge signals which alert the rest of the herd and with luck scare away the opposition. They are most often given by stallions as a challenge to other stallions. They are a sign of high excitement. Excitable domestic horses of both sexes snort at remarkable objects (pigs, people wearing exotic hats) especially when there is a conflict between the desire to investigate and the fear of strangeness; they also snort when they are feeling 'high' and are playing at being alarmed. American saddlebreds are particularly snorty; this is due to a combination of their extravagant and melodramatic temperament and the particular shape of their noses, which often leads to high blowing too.

Screams and roars are fortunately not often heard, as they are the cry of a horse in an extreme emotional state – usually of rage and fear, during fighting. Angry out-of-season mares may scream at persistent stallions; horses that are fighting seriously, not in play, scream and roar; but the most spine-chilling time to hear a scream is when a genuinely vicious horse has decided it is time to kill you.

Grunts are given during extreme effort, as in fighting, jumping and strug-gling to get up after a fall; they are also given in pain and distress, as in a foaling mare or in colic. They do not seem to be used deliberately as a signal.

Groans. Some horses groan a good deal when getting up, yawning or being mounted. This seems to signify that a great effort is being made, as we might by groaning at such times, and is not socially-directed.

Two other sounds that are neither calls nor socially-directed but that may indicate a horse's emotional state are:

High blowing, a gentle snorty noise, which is partly due to the shape of the nasal septum. Horses prone to high blowing often do it when pleasantly excited and feeling fresh, but they may also do it when cantering quietly and enjoying themselves.

Nose blowing, a pleasant relaxed sound, is the 'hrrrrmph' that a horse makes when walking home on a long rein after a good ride, or when he has settled and relaxed into his work. Horses also do it when loafing together. It is a sound to be welcomed as it signifies an easy, comfortable frame of mind. When a horse is clearly in that state you can often provoke him into nose blowing by imitating it yourself, and set up an exchange.

Some horses *snore* when they are fast asleep . . . .

Just as they generalize their social feelings, horses also generalize to include people in their communications. Since they call a good deal to each other, it is not surprising that they respond so readily to voice training. Their own softer noises, like nickering and nose-blowing, are comfortable and comforting, while the harsher scream and squeal are not; horses detest being shouted at, but an easy relaxed tone relaxes them too. Many horses obviously enjoy singing, soft whistling, and even the radio; whether certain types of music appeal to them naturally, or because of their interest value or pleasant associations, is not clear.

BODY POSTURE

An animal's body posture betrays its emotional state, and most social animals have developed specific signals based on this. Horses watch each other constantly for these signs of attitude.

Generally speaking, the more excited a horse is the more exciting her outline. Drowsy, relaxed horses doze with one hip aslant, ears drooping, head sagging, tail low. A highly excited horse presents a series of lively curves, with pricked ears, high head, arched neck, swelling muscles and high tail. This is especially seen in the *startle posture*, when one horse spots something alarming. At the sight of this tense, alert outline other horses become alert too (a few snorts may awake them even further) and, if the alarm proves noteworthy, quickly bunch together and poise ready for flight. A horse that is giving the alarm reinforces her 'startle' attitude by moving in a series of high, jerky steps, calling attention to herself still further.

SIGNS OF BODY TENSION ARE ALARM SIGNALS. Since horses tend to generalize their social feelings to include us, they interpret signs of body tension in people to be alarm signals too. Tense, frightened

Plate 11 *Playing* (see page 114) *in horses, as in other mammals, is a merry way of practising movements that in adult wild life are enacted for real in the deadly serious struggle for survival. Cats, dogs and other hunters play at hunting; hunted animals play at being hunted. Rabbits play at hide-and-seek and races; dolphins play at escape leaps; horses play at startles and running away. A particularly skittish and lively horse stops, tail up, looking for something to be startled at before high-tailing away in a melodramatic role of wild-horse-scared-by-a-snake. Other horses watching such a display become playfully excited too.*

people actually frighten horses and make them want to run away. It is true that some old, experienced horses do learn to take advantage of nervous beginners, but this happens less often than many people think: for the majority of horses the sight of stiff, jerky movements is simply a clear signal that there is something frightening nearby. If we have put ourselves in the position of leader in the relationship, the horse is doubly anxious: if we are fearful, so should he be. Combined with the fact that he cannot see the cause of the alarm, it is enough to make him dance about nervously, ready to take flight.

People (including novices) who have 'a way with horses' tend to move in a particularly relaxed, unhurried, non-jerky fashion that is reassuring to a horse and makes him want to stay near them. Many fierce horses, used to harsh handling, are astonishingly gentle with children, who tend to be relaxed.

The emphasis on *outline* as a potent form of signalling explains why the

Figure 13 *Body outlines signal a horse's state of arousal, and are sometimes used as particular signals. Curved outlines excite other horses, while smooth ones soothe them.*

1 The displaying stallion, his tail raised in excitement, swells his muscles and prances. His tucked-in head allows him to see near-range attractions.

2 The displaying mare, in typical saw-horse position, raises her tail attractively but keeps her ears back in the submissive position.

3 Relaxed horse rests on one hip, presenting a dull outline.

4 'Startle' posture, the most eye-catching of all, shows maximum curviness in the high head, pricked ears, arched neck, high tail and tense muscles. Movements in startle are high and jerky.

5 Herding stallion lowers his head, snaky-necking in threat to his mares, but lifts his feet high.

6 Dozing horse locks one stifle joint and rests on that hip, showing a minimum of excitement in her outline.

sight of a person, even a familiar one, wearing a hat or carrying an umbrella, a high rucksack or a bale of hay, often alarms horses: they look at our outlines rather than our features, and see a totally unfamiliar signal.

TAILS AND EARS

Tails and ears are good forms of signalling because they alter the horse's outline dramatically. As well as *high-tailing* in excitement, horses show *tail-flattening* in submission and fear: a frightened horse will put his tail right between his legs like a dog, and often scare himself into total panic as he feels it wrap snakily round his hocks (often seen when a horse has been mounted for the first time too early). Another sign of fear and anxiety is frequent *dunging* or even diarrhoea (e.g. horse approaching ramp of horsebox). In *movement* a horse carries his tail higher than at rest: he raises his tail just before moving, so it can be taken as a sign of intention to move. On the whole, the higher the tail, the more aroused the horse.

Tail movements are also used as signals. Tail *lashing* is a sign of annoyance and irritation, and is seen in frustration and conflict. Sometimes the irritation is caused by physical discomfort, as in colic or other internal pain. Horses in schooling often lash their tails slightly when asked to perform a movement they find particularly difficult, or one which has given trouble in the past. Angry horses lash their tails violently. This signal has probably developed from the normal use of the tail in whisking at irritating flies. A *kink in the tail* is seen in a tense horse who might like to lash his tail but is too tense to do so; it often precedes bucking.

In *jumping* a horse lifts his tail after his hindquarters; in bucking he usually lifts his tail first.

The high-tail = excitement signal is also used by in-season mares displaying to a stallion, but here it is combined with a lower head position and drooping ears, eliminating the possibility of its being a startle posture. To attract the stallion's interest still further, the mare (*a*) produces a particularly smelly urine and (*b*) winks her vulva at him to show her willingness to be mounted. Vulva-winking is a good signal because of the eye-catching colour contrasts involved.

Ear positions

'My horse looks with his ears,' a child once remarked, and ears are indeed the best indicators of where a horse's attention lies. Drooping ears indicate

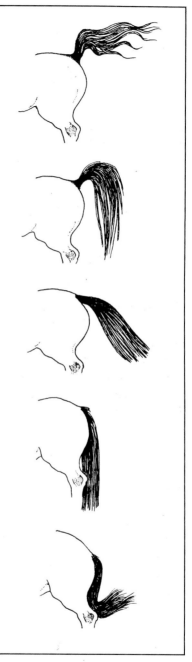

High tail: high excitement, as in stallion display in courtship or challenge, running away, play, excited greeting.

Milder arousal, as in greeting, approach/avoidance conflict, display (part of mare's courtship posture), investigation, excited fear, threat; also dunging.

Movement or intention to move or go faster; general alertness; urination.

Dullness: sleep, dozing, pain, sickness, being chased.

Unhappiness: submissive fear, defensive attack (about to kick in self-defence).

Figure 14 *Tail position varies according to the horse's state of excitement.*
(After Kiley-Worthington)

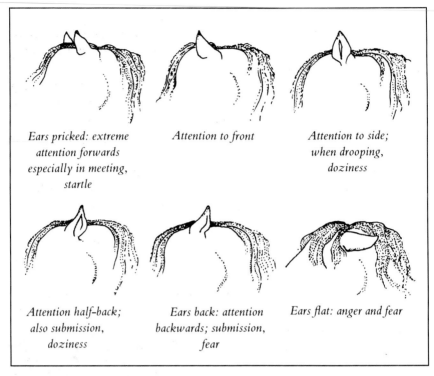

Figure 15 *Ear positions.*

non-attention, as in drowsiness; ears turned half-back and flat, indicate submission (but *see mouthing, opposite*), while alert ears turned in any direction show to what the horse is listening. Ears turned back are not necessarily a sign of temper, merely of attention focused backwards; a horse frightened from in front turns his ears back to hear what is behind him in case he may run backwards. But when a horse flattens his ears backwards it is a sure sign that he thinks he is liable to get into trouble, either through his own ill-will or somebody else's. Often the ears are pointed in different directions, indicating split attention.

MOUTHS AND NOSES

Ears and tails are clear forms of signalling because they alter the horse's outline. *Mouth movements* which draw the lips back, exposing the gums and teeth, are also high-contrast signals, as in the 'mouthing' of foals and in teeth-baring (threat to bite). The 'stallion smile' (Flehmen), the stallion's way of smelling an in-season mare's urine, is usually a prelude to growing sexual excitement, though whether other horses understand it as a signal for that is not clear. It is also seen in a non-sexual context in horses tasting or smelling something unexpected for the first time.

Mouthing. Young foals have a special submission signal, like the rolling over of a young puppy before its elders and betters: they droop their ears, stretch their necks, and make 'snapping' or 'mouthing' movements with the teeth exposed. Very young foals 'mouth' at anything big that moves (including bicycles); later they only do it when approaching (or approached by) an older horse. Later still, as yearlings, they start to lose the reaction and only do it when actually threatened by an older horse. The rate at which they lose the reaction depends on their maturity: well-grown, bold yearlings lose it altogether, but weedy, submissive youngsters continue to do it even until they are two-year-olds. As they stop doing it they are, in a way, showing their readiness to be treated as fully-fledged members of the herd (*see Appendix 1*).

Other *mouth movements* of a less dramatic kind are seen in horses that are relaxing after being tense. Tense horses tend to stiffen the jaw and neck

Plate 12 *Young foal 'mouthing' submissively at an adult mare. In fact, the mare's gentle expression shows that she has no intention of attacking although she is smelling the foal carefully.*

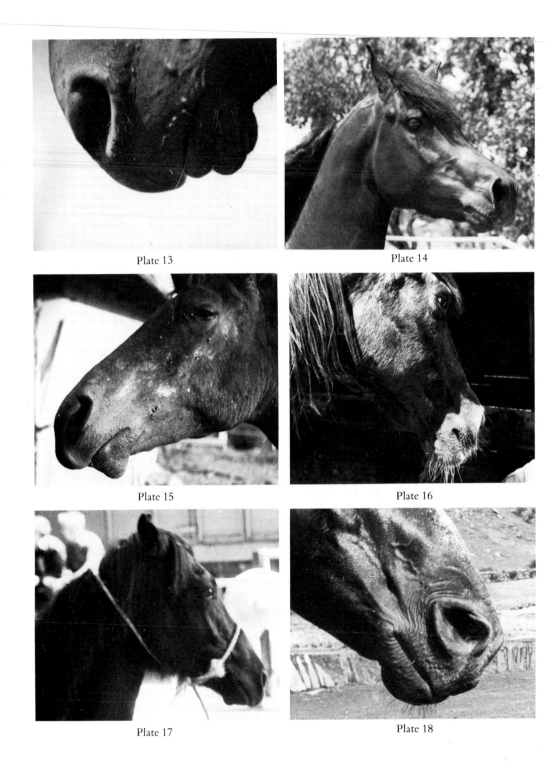

Plate 13

Plate 14

Plate 15

Plate 16

Plate 17

Plate 18

especially, and when the tension dies down they often make small munching movements, much as we wriggle our shoulders after they have been held stiffly.

The *tight mouth* of tension is shown in many different moods: in fear, upset, conflict, confusion and mild anger, all of which are unpleasant feelings. As the mouth gets tighter the chin dimples into a ball, and the nose starts to pull down over the teeth.

The complete opposite is the *saggy mouth* of a dozy, relaxed horse, seen especially in hot weather. Horses that are exhausted or in deep pain also have relaxed mouths but the flaring of their nostrils shows that they are

---

Plate 13 *Tight mouth of mild tension in this mare who does not want to meet another horse that is trying to reach her. This is the same mare as on page 73 where her relaxed, undimpled chin shows that she is in a better mood. Here she is grumpy and disapproving.*

Plate 14 *Shakertown in a conflict: he has just been trying to court a mare that did not want to be courted and kicked out at him. He shows signs of acute tension in his tight mouth and long nose; of arousal in his flared nostrils; and of confusion in his wayward ears, one of which listens to the mare while the other checks behind him. The stiffness in his neck betrays his tension too.*

Plate 15 *Long nose without tension shown by Ranger, who is in a state of ecstasy while his withers are being scratched. Although his nose is stretched his nostrils, mouth and chin are relaxed and his half-closed eyes have a dreamy expression.*

Plate 16 *Severe pain. Triangle of stress, a deep groove above this old mare's mouth, seems to contradict her saggy, relaxed lip. But her slightly flared nostril (indicating arousal) and pricked, alert ears (unfortunately out of the picture) show that she was wide awake, although her dull, unseeing eye does not seem so. In fact she was in agony from a severe attack of laminitis and was put down soon after this photo was taken. People in severe pain also show the same contradictory signs of relaxed mouth, stress round the nostrils, and unfocusing eyes.*

A horse in such severe pain often sweats patchily, especially on the face and shoulder, but as she does not move about the sweat does not wet the coat until you put your hand on it. Terrified horses sweat in this way too.

Plate 17 *Characteristic stiff neck and tight mouth of tense fear in this scared youngster. Note the 'triangle of stress' appearing above his mouth due to his slightly flared nostrils.*

Plate 18 *Irritation. Lipizzan stallion Maestoso Sitnica wrinkles his nose in annoyance at the idea of having to go inside on a chilly night. The white streak and bone thickenings on his nose are from old extensive injuries (chain? cavesson?). A horse in mild pain, from colic for instance, also wrinkles his nose in irritation like this.*

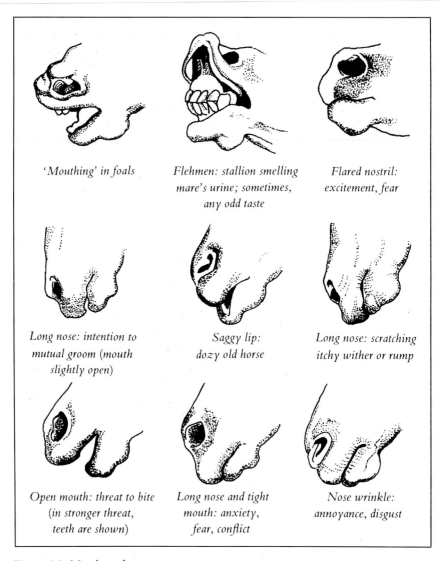

'Mouthing' in foals

Flehmen: stallion smelling
mare's urine; sometimes,
any odd taste

Flared nostril:
excitement, fear

Long nose: intention to
mutual groom (mouth
slightly open)

Saggy lip:
dozy old horse

Long nose: scratching
itchy wither or rump

Open mouth: threat to bite
(in stronger threat,
teeth are shown)

Long nose and tight
mouth: anxiety,
fear, conflict

Nose wrinkle:
annoyance, disgust

Figure 16 Mouths and noses.

not asleep: they are withdrawn, sunk into themselves, in contrast to the
tight-mouthed tense horse.

The *chin* can be dimpled without the mouth being tense, as is seen
particularly in the expression of a mare who is willing to be mated and is
waiting for the stallion to mount her.

While a long nose wrapped over a tight mouth shows tension, and often
fear, horses pull long noses in other moods too: when they are reaching

out for things, or when they are expectant, eager or playful. Here the mouth is not tense, the chin not dimpled. Some horses have particularly mobile noses which they use very expressively: Shakertown, for instance, wears a long nose kinked to one side whenever he is in a playfully energetic mood.

A *long nose* wiggling about freely is a prelude to scratching, rolling, and searching in people's pockets. Horses intending to mutual groom approach each other with these questing noses, usually opening their mouths a little as they do so, and quickly turn to fastening them on each other's withers in an ecstasy of being scratched. 'If a horse is much tickled,' Darwin noted, 'as when curry combed, his wish to bite something becomes so intolerably strong that he will clatter his teeth together and, though not vicious, bite his groom.'

Nostrils can be extremely expressive, especially in the thin-skinned breeds. *Flared nostrils* are a sign of arousal, usually in fear or startle but also in play; they are flared in panting, too, but then of course they move with each breath. *Nose-wrinkling*, when the back margin of the nostril is flared backwards so that a wrinkle appears behind it, is a sign of annoyance, either at pain or at some other irritation, and may be used in the mildest form of threat; the ears are then back. A mating mare also wrinkles her nostrils when she dimples her chin, putting her ears in the half-back position as she stands in the saw-horse posture. Whether she is irritated by the stallion behind her, or merely trying to smell him without turning her head, is not clear.

HEAD MOVEMENTS

The most well-defined of these, used as a signal, is the *head thrust*, where the nose is tipped abruptly forwards and upwards with a jerk of the neck. It is an aggressive threat movement, and is the commonest form of threat between horses. The ears are flattened and the mouth may be opened in a threat to bite. Carried further, it becomes a *lunge* of the whole body or even, in extreme rage, a fully-fledged *charge*.

The *nudge*, a slower and gentler movement, does not carry the head upwards, and the ears are not flattened but are half-back or forward. It is an attention-seeking movement: loafing horses nudge their friends to move them or to start mutual grooming, and a friendly horse in pain from colic or in foaling will nudge her handler in her distress.

*Head bob: trying to
see, especially oddity
in middle distance*

*Jerk-back: withdrawal,
out of fear or dislike; when
ridden or driven: jibbing, refusal*

Nudge: attention-seeking

*Head thrust:
aggressive threat*

*Head shake (head and neck): removing dust and flies;
when head held higher: annoyance, frustration*

Swing: away from threat to head

Nose shake (slow): what a fine fellow I am

Figure 17 *Head movements.*

Head shakes are the horse's natural way of getting rid of annoying flies
and shaking herself free of dust, as after rolling; they are also used in all
kinds of annoying or frustrating conditions that the horse would like to
free herself of. A horse that wants to bite you but dare not, or a horse that
cannot get at her food or her friends, will shake her head. Horses that are
annoyed by the bit, or by being ridden at all, also shake their heads, or toss

them, or develop their own habitual mixture of the two. High-spirited horses sometimes flap their bottom lips in mild annoyance at the bit too.

A *nose shake*, where the poll stays in the same place but the nose swings briefly and slowly to one or both sides, is given especially by stallions showing off in display or playing at it; some horses also do it when they have just completed a task requiring boldness and are stepping out gaily afterwards.

The *jerk-back* is a sharp backwards and upwards movement away from something frightening – a threat from a horse or a person. Carried further, it becomes a rear: a young horse that tends to stop and jerk back is a potential rearer. Half-asleep horses also jerk their heads as they nod off, or to dislodge flies: the latter is a mild form of *head-tossing* which has the same 'annoyance' connotation as head-shaking but is less often used in frustration.

The *head bob*, a rapid ducking movement, goes with pricked ears and intent stares. It is the horse's attempt to look at middle-distance objects whose size puzzles him.

 ## NECK MOVEMENTS

A *neck swing* carries the head away from danger without the 'backwardness' inherent in the jerk-back. A stallion trying to court a mare swings his head away when the mare threatens to kick him; a horse that dislikes a hand on his face does the same.

Snaky-necking, when the head is held very low, outstretched, and wobbled from side to side on a sinuous neck, is the stallion's way of herding his mares. Young colts sometimes herd other animals, like sheep

Figure 18 *Neck-wringing*.

and chickens, in this way, and if they catch up with them may stamp on them; aggressive mares sometimes chase dogs in this way too.

Neck-wringing is a peculiar contorted movement of the neck such that the head is thrown all over the place. While it can be seen in normal horses in play, it is usually seen in rather aggressive but indecisive horses: a stallion not bold enough to confront an enemy forcefully, a ridden horse that hates the whole process yet will not rebel honestly. It is more common in Arabs and is an unhappy, sinister action since the horse makes himself blind, partly deaf, and totally uncoordinated in front while he is doing it.

BODY MOVEMENTS

There are of course hundreds of ways that a horse can move his body, and some of these have special signal value.

The *body check*, where one horse swings across in front of another, prevents the second horse from moving forward and is a threat. The *shoulder-barge* is a body check carried into contact, and is an action encouraged in polo ponies to ride each other off.

Rump presentation is the mildest form of threat to kick, and is only too familiar to people who have horses that are hard to catch.

Elevated movements of all kinds are a sign of excitement.

LEGS

Legs can signal too. The *hindleg lift*, which may follow rump presentation, is a slightly stronger threat to kick.

The *foreleg strike* is a rapid, high flick of the foreleg often seen when two horses meet. The horse often squeals at the same time: both are warnings to the second horse to keep his distance and not be too familiar.

Figure 19 *Foreleg strike.*

Plate 19 *Furious little stallion paws in frustration at not being able to reach the mares behind me. Note, however, that he is making no attempt to get away. The abundant mane on these little native ponies is good protection in the winter: hot-blooded horses have much thinner manes. Llanybythyr market.*

Pawing is often used to get at or investigate things: to move snow off grass; to break ice; to raise dust before rolling. It is also a sign of frustration, and is seen in horses prevented from getting at the object of their desire. Some horses lift a foreleg while eating; this is a very mild form of pawing, and here the frustration seems to lie in the fact that the horse cannot stuff food down himself as fast as he would like.

THREAT SIGNALS

Like other social animals horses do have things to argue about, and as far as possible they try to resolve their differences by threat rather than fighting. There are two forms of threat:

1. *aggressive (attacking) threat*, where the horse deliberately attacks another horse (or person). This is given head-on.
2. *defensive threat*, where the horse wishes to defend himself against a presumed attack from another animal. This is given rear-end on.

Defensive threat, which may turn to defensive attack if the horse feels that that is the only way to rid himself of his enemy, has an element of fear rather than rage; in aggressive threat or attack it is the other way round. It is noticeable that most of the threats that horses present to people are defensive ones. Both forms of threat can be given in increasing strengths.

Table 6 *Aggressive threat*

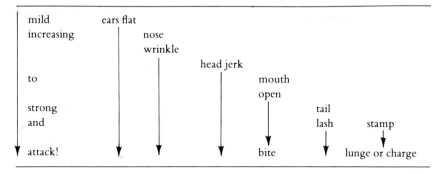

mild increasing	ears flat	nose wrinkle	head jerk	mouth open	tail lash	stamp
to						
strong and					tail lash	
attack!	↓	↓	↓ bite	↓	↓	↓ lunge or charge

Figure 20 *Aggressive threat series.*

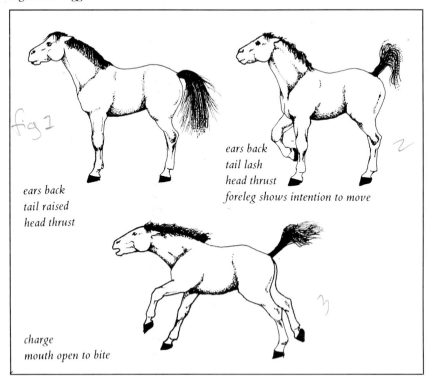

ears back
tail raised
head thrust

ears back
tail lash
head thrust
foreleg shows intention to move

charge
mouth open to bite

Table 7 *Defensive threat*

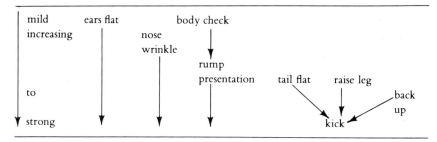

Figure 21 *Defensive threat series.*

ears back
tail flat
rump presentation

showing a foot:
threat to kick

the final defence: kicking

Figure 22 *Kicking, or 'defensive attack', is the horse's final defence against an animal she feels is attacking her although this feeling may not be justified. It is commoner in mare fights than stallion fights. The other horse swings his head and prepares to jump his forequarter away to avoid the kick.*

Submission When a threatened horse wishes to admit defeat, he turns away with ears half-back or drooping. In a threat-fight, the first to turn away is the loser.

6

Self Protection

RUNNING AWAY

This is the horse's natural defence, his instant reaction whenever he feels afraid, threatened, startled, or even just faced with something he does not understand. In the wild, horses that escape accidents and starvation are in danger mainly from wolves, lions and snakes, which they cannot fight. In the Abruzzi mountains of central Italy, wolves kill pastured horses more often than they kill cows: a cornered cow can defend herself quite adequately with her horns, but a horse cannot. Horses must run away.

Nowadays, even for wild ones, there are far fewer predators than there were at the time when horses evolved; but the selection pressures that shaped the horse's survival programmes favoured running away so strongly that even today the reaction is fast, automatic, and fundamental to the horse's whole psychology. To work as a method of self-defence, running away must be easy to set off, and start without a moment's hesitation: this is exactly what we find. For an animal that does not catch its food, there is no point in running towards sounds of a strange animal, but the small chance that it may be a tiger means that it is always worth while running away. We tend to interpret this as meaning that horses are very fearful creatures since we, as semi-predators, tend to check on the noise first and only run away when we are frightened. Horses, however, run away first, even when they are merely startled.

In the herd, once a serious alarm is given the whole group bunches together as it takes to flight. In the panic of a true stampede horses can barely see where they are going, and in strange territory they may run themselves into difficulty. In their own country they know the safe paths, and as the panic dies down they tend to string out, though they may go on for quite a distance before they eventually stop.

Plate 20 *Welsh mountain pony running away, startled, one ear on the disturbance and one on her foal. In a typical display of 'startle' she raises her tail and lifts her feet high, her neck and mouth tight with tension. Other ponies nearby would become alarmed at these signs even if they had seen no reason for them, and would start to run too.*

The high spirit and good lines of this grand little mare are evident despite her poor condition: carrying one foal and feeding another, she has just triumphed through the worst winter in sixty years high in the mountains. Trawsfynydd.

Smaller disturbances lead to shorter flights before the horse whisks round to face the 'danger' and identify it. Any movement near or behind a horse may be a threat, and unless he has learned otherwise he will make one of these shorter flights. If he cannot run away the horse will turn to face the threat; if he cannot even do that he may be forced to resort to defending himself by kicking. Kicking out at an attacker endangers the back legs (wolves tend to bring their victims down by hamstringing them) and horses do not do it unless their other methods of self-defence have been removed from them: a wild horse loose in a pen will not kick a man unless the man forces him to do so.

FEET

No foot, no 'oss. (R. S. Surtees, *Jorrocks*)

To run away you need good feet: one of the horse's strongest built-in survival programmes says *look after your feet*. Anything that threatens a horse's feet by implication threatens his life and, as with running away, it is better to be safe than sorry. Horses are extremely careful to avoid anything that might possibly threaten their feet, which includes any new and untested surface; they are greatly reassured if they can see another horse, or any animal, walking on it safely. Among the usual things that frighten horses at first are:

streams and puddles (which might conceal any kind of horror);

marshy and boggy land, and soft sand;

anything round the feet (ropes, hands, wire);

hollow-sounding bridges and ramps (which might give way);

shadows on a bright smooth surface;

white road-lines;

crumbliness underfoot;

jumps, especially when not on a path, for the landing cannot be seen;

treading on anything that might move, especially anything live. (The efforts that racehorses make to avoid treading on fallen jockeys are remarkable.)

Other patterns of behaviour naturally follow from the 'look after your feet' premise. Horses prefer to follow each other, for if the leader's feet are safe then so are the followers'. They prefer to use paths, which represent lines of past safety between unknown perils: horses loose in strange country will sniff out paths. Thus young horses which are afraid of being ridden on to a new type of surface will readily follow another horse's lead, or will follow a person on foot.

CONFINEMENT AND RESTRAINT

To a naturally free-ranging animal like the horse confinement is at first terrifying, for it removes all possibility of self-defence by running away. As natural cave-dwellers, finding comfort and security in small, snug places, we often find this difficult to understand: we provide barns and shelters, only to find that horses seldom use them except to escape from flies in hot weather. In vile winter weather horses stand backed up under a hedge or wall, tails tucked in. Though they look miserable, they prefer to be outside, free. **HORSES ARE NATURALLY CLAUSTRO-PHOBIC.**

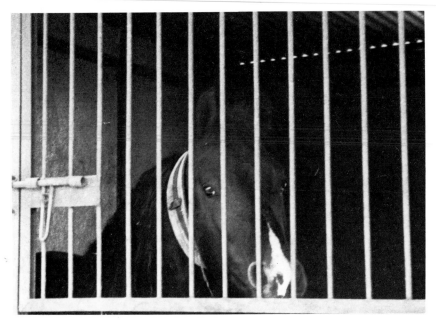

Plate 21 *'All who had to do with me were good, and I had a light, airy stable and the best of food. What more could I want? Why, liberty!' Anna Sewell,* Black Beauty

Many horses learn to accept confinement, and many have known no-thing else, but there are some, often the more active and intelligent ones, for whom the oppression of being imprisoned against their nature is too heavy a strain. Many horses kept in such unnatural conditions, deprived of freedom, exercise and companions, become excitable, irritable or 'stupid'. Their behaviour patterns do not equip them for this way of life: psycho-logically they are fish out of water. How much of this unhappiness is due to being cooped up and how much to other causes is difficult to sort out but there is no doubt that being shut inside is one of them. Ask any horse; give him the choice, and he will choose his freedom. Where a horse has to be kept inside, turning him out for even a few hours often has an almost magical effect on his temper and nature. But few horses really have to be kept inside: usually it is our demands and ideals that imprison them.

Fear of entering small, enclosed spaces like horseboxes and trailers can be helped by making them appear as large as possible: open windows and doors create an illusion of space. Given the choice, most horses turn round in a trailer so that they can see out of the back. From the horse's point of view it is a pity we do not design horseboxes with large windows, and compartments facing backwards (*see also page 187*).

Being restrained in any way is at first a traumatic experience for a horse, though most habituate to it soon. It is especially terrible for an adult wild horse to find his head restrained for the first time, and even well-domesticated horses are frightened by being held tightly unless they are used to it. Leading a horse on a loose rope allows him to move his head to see anything he wants, but on a tight lead or rein the horse is forced to hold his head in a position where he cannot see his feet nor move his head to look at oddities. A horse in a panic is often quietened by giving him a little more rein and space, not less: he can then turn to look at whatever is bothering him. It is also a fearful experience for a horse to be ridden over rough country on a short rein, for he cannot see where his feet are; many refuse to move at all unless they can move their heads up and down freely. Small ponies that are unused to being handled dislike being led close by an adult, for they cannot see your head if you are too near. In all these cases the natural fear of restraint is compounded by the problems of seeing properly and an understandable lack of faith in the handler or rider.

Grabbing at a horse's head, even that of an old and tame one, makes

Plate 22 *A restraining hand prevents this young Arab stallion from being able to turn and look at what is disturbing him (a rude photographer), so he has to cock an ear and roll his eye to do the best he can. Being held tight in this crowded, noisy market made him afraid because he could not see, and he rolled his eyes more and more wildly.*

him shy away: a quiet, friendly horse will allow us to throw an arm around his neck but not make the same movement towards his head. The innate fear of having the head restrained is so basic as to break through years of training and trust.

The ultimate form of restraint for a horse is to be made legless so he has no chance of running away. Sitting on a fallen horse's neck prevents him from getting up (he has to raise his head before he can roll on to his feet) and makes him instantly submissive. Some of the older methods of breaking used this to subdue horses that had grown impossible to handle, for the horse's dislike of total powerlessness is so strong as to make him learn his limitations rapidly. Such methods are horribly dangerous and unnecessary anyway, but if by chance a horse throws himself off his feet by behaving riotously, it is worth sitting on his head for a while to let him think about the consequences.

7

Living

How do these sociable, defenceless animals come into existence, live and die?

BREEDING

In natural conditions there is likely to be a shortage of food in the winter months, and the best time for foals to be born is in early summer when grass is at its most nutritious. The normal length of pregnancy in a horse is about 11 months; mares, then, should only mate during the spring and summer months. This is taken care of by one of those wonderfully simplistic biological arrangements: native mares are only fertile when the day is longer than the night, that is, between the March and September equinoxes, for the hormones that give rise to ovulation are light-controlled.

The male sex hormone, testosterone, is also influenced by the length of day. During winter stallions are fertile but do not usually show an urgent desire for sex, but around the spring equinox they change visibly, putting on weight around the cresty neck and muscular shoulders and behaving generally in a more stallion-like manner as their sex drive increases. These hormonal changes can be produced artificially by giving extra light to stabled horses in the winter, so that the breeding season can be started earlier.

Heat

During heat most mares show distinct behaviour changes, though there are great individual differences. The main sign of heat is frequent, nervous-looking urination, with a good deal of vulva-winking and tail-

Plate 23 *'Winking' of an in-season mare shows a sudden, eye-catching flash of pink as she displays her willingness to be mated. The thoroughbred mare in the background is lazily blowing her nose. Nantmor.*

raising, especially to stallions but also to any strange horse. Some mares become flighty or irritable; others rub themselves sensually against friends; a few become what can only be described as sex-mad, expecting to be mated every time someone climbs on their back; and others never 'show' at all. During the first couple of days most behave capriciously, 'showing' to a stallion and then turning to kick and squeal when he attempts to come near, but as the heat deepens they become willing, and even eager, to be mounted.

Most mares come into heat for about 5 days every 3 weeks, ovulating on the next to last day of heat. They are even less regular than women, though: some mares have longer heats, some shorter and some have longer non-heat periods. Barren mares later in the season often show prolonged heats lasting up to 40 days, and some mares show 'split' heats.

Figure 23 *Courting stallion raises his tail in excitement, tucks his nose in so that he can see the close-range attraction, arches his neck impressively and prances while he makes up his mind to move in closer to the mare. However, his long, forceful nickers seem to be what melts her heart.*

Courtship

In the natural course of events a stallion will not mount an unwilling mare, nor even show much interest in her except as a herd-member, until she starts soliciting, drifting past his nose and winking provocatively as she goes. Stimulated by her uplifted tail and the smell of her urine, he shows Flehmen, nickers forcefully, and often prances about in an elevated manner with arched neck, performing piaffes and passages that would grace the Spanish Riding School. These steps are a kind of stallion's courtship dance, the high action and curved silhouette showing his interest and excitement and also his conflict. For mating a mare can be a dangerous business: invading another animal's personal space is against social training. Like many animals the stallion may find himself caught in an approach/avoidance conflict, circling the dangerous, desirable goal until the signs of the mare's willingness are unmistakable. Courtship varies considerably according to the experience of both partners, their hormonal state, and their relative success with each other, but it consists of an exchange of moves and signals that finally persuade the mare to stand still while the stallion mates her. His long, low nickers may be enough persuasion, but he may also start grooming her neck and withers, scratching, rubbing and nuzzling at her, working his way back to her flanks. When she allows him near her rump he stands to one side to avoid kicks and sniffs, licks, nibbles and nips at her tail and back legs, showing Flehmen and nickering as he does so. As his excitement grows he becomes erect. At any point the mare may find his attention too forceful and stamp, kick or squeal, which generally sends him dancing in his circles; or the mare too may break from her 'saw-horse' stance and start high-stepping about before stopping and urinating again. But if she is really ready the mare will stand still, her back braced, her tail raised to one side, 'showing' again while he comes behind and to one side of her, rubbing her rump with his shoulder.

Mating

When the stallion finally mounts he does not necessarily achieve his goal straight away: often he gets himself tangled up in her tail and has to withdraw and start again, while a young mare may walk forward when

Plate 24 *Maestoso loafing on a spring afternoon. As hormone levels rise in early spring, masturbation is not uncommon in lone stallions. Maestoso's interest may have been caught by wishful thinking about a distant sheep: there are no mares around, and his jenny donkey, who is behind him, does not arouse him sexually although she does her best to solicit him when she is in season. Most stallions take no interest in jennies, although jacks readily mate mares.*

his weight comes on her. The stallion may hold the mare's shoulder in his teeth when he mounts, but the savage biting seen in many domestic stallions does not seem to be a normal part of the mutual agreement of mating. Copulation lasts between 5 and 60 seconds usually. The stallion shows pelvic thrusts and usually flags his tail as he ejaculates. A vigorous stallion is ready to mate again within ten minutes or so if the mare solicits him, but usually the pair drift apart and mate again later that day. A demanding mare will not only display to a tired stallion but also excite him by nibbling and licking at his sheath.

Mares in a harem seek out the stallion when they are ready, and mares running loose where there are less than the normal number of stallions also look for a mate at the right time, as is seen in many native ponies kept on the hills. Domestic mares, too, sometimes go so far as to break out of their pasture to search for a stallion when they are in season, and when ridden tend to display hopefully to any strange horse, stallion or not.

In the unnatural conditions in which many stallions are kept they often become over-eager and even vicious towards mares, while keen young stallions may find themselves hurt, bewildered, and frightened to try again. Mares, too, may become discouraged and refuse to stand even when fully in season because the normal courtship cannot take place and the necessary signals have not been exchanged. Many stud horses have not been raised with a group anyway, so their social manners and ability to use the language of signals may be sadly lacking; some stallions practically rape mares and others find it difficult to mate at all. This creates a rising spiral of difficulties, for the horses may be literally dangerous to each other and have to be restrained in such a way that a successful mating becomes even less likely. For this normal pattern of signals to lead to a harmonious mating both horses should:

(a) have been raised with a group, so that they know the language;
(b) have enough time and space to be able to use it properly;
(c) be in the right hormonal state.

Although mares will only mate when fully in season, this does not necessarily mean that their hormonal levels are high enough for them to be able to conceive and hold to service. It is commonly accepted that a mare that will not come in season, or will not hold when mated in hand, will often become pregnant when running out with a stallion: she needs to smell him regularly for her hormones to function properly. Although there seems to be litttle research on horses on this point, chemical messages or pheromones are well known to be controllers of hormone levels in many social animals. Recent Australian research on pigs, for instance, has shown that their sex hormones do not reach reasonable levels if they are kept isolated, or raised in isolation; but it is not clear whether the effect is due to pheromones or to social contact.

All in all, it is barely surprising that horses, which normally have a rich social life, have great problems with this most social of acts in abnormal conditions. One study of Welsh ponies showed that in closely related strains less than 65 per cent of mares became pregnant when mated in hand, whereas over 90 per cent of them did when running on the hill with a stallion for the same length of time; another study of Hanoverians gives 50 per cent as the average foaling rate.

Even in the wild, though, there may be difficulties. A jealous and aggressive mare may prevent other mares from mating even when she is not in season herself, by chasing them away from the stallion or by simply standing in front of him, guarding him. Many stallions show colour prejudice. Hope Ryder noted a stallion in Montana whose entire harem, an exceptionally large one, consisted of bay mares; one Nevada mustang only has buckskins, while the black Lipizzaner (*see page 125*) prefers light-coloured mares and will even attempt to mate pale geldings. Darwin commented that 'half-wild horses apparently prefer to pair with those of the same colour', but it may be truer to say that they prefer mares the colour of their dams, or their playmates: we do not know. Sometimes stallions take absolutely no interest in certain mares. Darwin states: 'The famous Monarque, for instance, would never consciously look at the dam of Gladiateur, and a trick had to be practised.'

Pregnancy

Once a mare is pregnant her behaviour settles to a more placid, though also more defensive, mode. Pregnant domestic mares kept without a stallion may become very aggressive towards any passing males, lashing their tails and even squirting urine in a way which makes one wonder if they are coming into season again, though they are not. A few mares do show seasons in pregnancy. Later in pregnancy most mares become sluggish and even positively dreamy.

Birth

The length of pregnancy varies between 340 and 350 days in domestic horses but appears to be longer in wild horses. In New Forest ponies 27 per cent foaled in 336 to 364 days, 67 per cent in 365 to 392 days, and 9 per

Table 8 *How much is a mare reacting to the sight, and how much to the sound, of the stallion?*

A large number of mares, either barren, with a foal at foot, or maidens, were tested to see what their reaction to a recording of a stallion's courtship nicker was in comparison to their reaction to the stallion himself. The left-hand figure in each column is the number of times the mares reacted to the recording alone, while the right-hand figure is the number of times they reacted to the stallion. The percentage efficiency of the sound recording compared to the stallion is also given.

Reactions of in-season mares

	Barren (77 tests)	Percentage efficiency of sound recording	Foal at foot (102 tests)	Percentage efficiency of sound recording	Maiden (32 tests)	Percentage efficiency of sound recording
standing	72/74	97	86/98	88	27/27	100
raising tail	67/73	92	82/87	85	26/24	108
winking	58/72	81	55/94	59	18/24	75
spreading hindlegs	54/72	75	55/93	57	18/25	72
urinating	36/55	58	36/64	56	10/24	42

Reactions of mares out of season

	(104 tests)		(80 tests)		(30 tests)	
'nervous'	88/102	86	76/80	95	26/30	87
kicking	1/100		3/80		0/29	
squealing	0/28		0/14		0/16	

The sound of the stallion was enough to make the mares stop in their tracks and show the first signs of their willingness as if to attract him. However, when the stallion did not appear many did not complete the display, although about a third of them did. The barren, experienced mares were altogether easier to arouse than the maidens. The non-oestrous (out of season) mares again behaved as if the stallion was there, though lacking his physical presence they had nothing to kick and squeal at.

The same experimenters tried to test the effectiveness of neck-pinching the mare, to mimic the stallion's biting the neck, and concluded that it actually put the mares off. People who have watched horses mating would disagree. It is probably very difficult to mimic the bite convincingly, and it is easy to see that a mistimed bite might be off-putting. Biting seems to make the mare arch her spine upwards, instead of squatting, and to make her lift her tail more, but there is generally so much going on that it is difficult to tell what causes what – hence these experiments.

(*Source: Veeckman & Odberg, 1978*)

cent in more than that. It is, of course, difficult to tell when a wild or feral horse has become pregnant. In Welsh ponies kept in natural conditions on the hills the length of pregnancy varies with the time of year, so that early-foalers go up to a month over time while late-foalers have theirs up to a month early, and this seems to be common especially in native breeds.

At foaling time, which in over 90 per cent of cases, wild or domestic, is in the early hours of the morning, the mare separates herself from the rest of the herd. This may be deliberate, or the result of getting left behind while the others move on. Like cows, some mares head for marshy places, ditches or ponds, drowning the foal by giving birth straight into water. Whether this highly non-adaptive behaviour occurs at all in the wild, or whether it is commoner in certain breeds, or in first-foalers is not documented. However, it is worth remembering when choosing a field for a mare to foal in.

Signs of discomfort – pawing, sweating, restless shifting about, looking at flanks – are followed by the waters bursting, when the mare usually lies down. Often she licks at the waters and Flehms. She may get up and down several times, but almost invariably she lies down for the birth itself, which is very rapid (5 – 45 minutes, usually 20). Birth is a private affair, and mares do not like company when they are giving birth. They are capable of retaining the foal for hours if necessary, waiting for the moment when they are alone, when the watchers have nipped off for a quick cup of coffee, to deliver it. Occasionally domestic mares call their handlers back to them so that they are not alone, but these cases are rare: as a rule, mares want to be alone.

Unless she is exhausted or bewildered, as first-foalers or horses that are being distracted sometimes are, the mare almost immediately nickers to the foal and starts licking him as he breaks out of the bag in which he is born. The foal responds to her call immediately too, flopping muzzily in the direction of her nicker. The mare's licking teaches her his individual smell, which is to play such an important part in her recognition of him in the months to come.

Like the young of most hoofed mammals, a healthy foal is wide awake and on his wobbly legs within half an hour or so, and beginning to show that first, magical, innate searching for a reward he has never known: milk. His hot, wet touch on the teat is a direct stimulus for the release of the hormone that triggers milk let-down (and which also stimulates more uterine contractions that help to expel the afterbirth).

The afterbirth, or cleansings, is passed an hour or two after the birth and the mare usually lies down again for this painful process. She does not eat the afterbirth.

Most mares help to direct the foal's first nuzzlings but some – usually they are first-foalers – reject their foals to varying degrees, even striking out at them with the forefeet. In the wild this has not been seen but in domestic horses it is by no means uncommon. Many such mares are of course completely unused to small foals, whereas a young wild mare is accustomed to having them fooling around her, so social experience no doubt has a good deal to do with it. There are also a few mares that accept their foals but are so ticklish underneath that they are reluctant to let them feed at first.

Mares are protective of their young foals and drive off other horses that come too near at first; domestic horses may also do this to their handlers.

FOAL BEHAVIOUR

The newborn foal matures astonishingly fast as his survival programmes become activated one by one. Within an hour he is standing, walking, feeding in more or less the right place, responding to his mother's nicker; an hour later he will have mastered cantering, following, keeping his place at his mother's flank, and will squeak his distress if he loses her. By the following afternoon he can walk, trot and gallop, whisk his tail at flies, get up and lie down in a coordinated manner, start nibbling at grass and piles of dung (these infect him with the necessary bacteria for his herbivorous gut) and begin, rather twitchily, to play.

In thoroughbred foals born under unnatural conditions a few foals have 'barking' fits not long after birth and the behaviour of these foals does not develop naturally. In severe cases they are known as dummies, for they simply sit wide-eyed, apparently insensible; later they may develop sight, and the ability to lie down, but in many cases they pass through a 'wandering' phase where they can hear, turn their heads to sound, walk, and get up, though they cannot lie down, suckle or follow. The independence of the patterns which make up normal behaviour is more clearly evident in such foals as they gradually develop one new action after another and so return to normality (*Rossdale*). *Isolation* of a young foal from birth results in total confusion of his social reactions: although he displays his own signals according to his own state, he cannot respond to those of others. The normal following, leading to imprinting (*see page 43*) and identity-recognition, are lost. Grzimek noted that foals isolated for the first two months of their lives were terrified when first introduced to horses.

Young foals spend a good deal of their time sleeping; feeding (about 4 times an hour), playing and investigating occupy the rest. During the first

Figure 24   *The young foal, exploring slightly outside his mother's space, feels a little uncertain. His attention is directed back towards her although he still faces away from her, while she keeps an eye and an ear on him.*

month they play mostly around their mothers, nibbling and pawing at them, and already developing the acute awareness of space and social distance that is characteristic of older horses as their mothers warn them not to stray too far. Later they move further away to play more with other foals, usually those of their own sex, racing, chasing, bucking, leaping and wrestling (*see play, page 114*). Even in the first couple of weeks colts show erection and playful mounting behaviour.

Exploration and investigation of their surroundings is important too: foals investigate mostly with their mouths at first, later tending to paw at strange objects. During the first few weeks foals are inquisitive and fearless, so that their mothers have to call them away from dangers; as the months go by they become increasingly mistrustful of anything strange.

Nibbling at grass and twigs, and *drinking*, are gradually perfected. At first foals have to bend their front legs to reach the ground.

Following persists as a strong response for the first year.

Social awareness becomes more marked: the 'mouthing' reaction of sub-mission to older horses develops, and foals show clearly that they learn the meaning of threat and startle, of the various calls, and of the differences between individuals in their group.

Mother-foal recognition Young foals straying from their mothers come hurtling back at the sound of a nicker, but they do not recognize the mother's call individually. Nor do they necessarily recognize their mothers; they are apt to run up to any horse of the same colour and even to try suckling from her. It is the mother who turns away the wrong foal, apparently by smell: mares always turn to touch their noses on the foals' bodies. Mares will not adopt strange foals unless the smell of them has been disguised or unless they are particularly maternal mares. (Sheep are similar: lambs will scurry at the sound of their mother's voice, but often go to the wrong ewe, only to be rebuffed when she smells them. Lambs with black mothers will often run hopefully up to a black dog, too.)

Weaning usually takes place when the next foal arrives. If the mare misses a year her yearling will go on suckling. Artificial weaning is usually done at about 6 months, when the foal is forcefully removed. At this time halter-breaking is relatively easy, since the foal readily transfers his following reaction to his handler; if, moreover, the foal has been caught and handled several times during the first week of life, when he can be led alongside his mother, he will remember the feeling of having his head restrained and be less liable to panic. (Otherwise the first tug on the rope tends to lead instantly to a backwards jerk of the head or of the whole body; it is easy for a foal to flip over backwards and break his neck.) A foal isolated at weaning time is bewildered, afraid and lonely.

Growing up in a Group

Growing up in a group involves gradual changes in social status. At first, young foals are merely part of their mothers, since they stay within their personal space. As they move about, however, they learn to avoid other horses' spaces and to respect adult horses. Later, in playing with other foals, they evolve their own social groups, and form friendships like adult horses. In their second year they begin to lose the 'mouthing' reaction that signals submission to older animals, and take up their positions as the weakest members of the group.

Throughout their first year, behaviour differences between colts and fillies gradually become more marked. Colts are rowdier and bolder than fillies, and tend to strike out with the front feet, rear and bite much more

Plate 25 *Yearling colts playing grown-up games. Mounting behaviour is not uncommon in colts' play and gives practice they appreciate in later years.*

than fillies. As they approach sexual maturity their play-fights become more frequent and serious, showing the components of adult stallion-fights: biting at the neck (windpipe and jugular vein), biting behind the elbows to force an opponent to his knees, rearing and striking, are all shown. When they start behaving in an openly sexual manner towards mares, the stallion chases them out of the herd so that they hover dejectedly on the outskirts.

These two-year-old colts are not alone, though. Either in their band or in another one the same thing is happening to others. Friends will leave their parent band together; lone colts meet other lone colts, and so bachelor groups are formed. Within each group there will be one colt stronger than the others, and if he has established his superiority clearly enough it will be he who claims the first filly they find and drives her away from the others to start his own band.

Young fillies' fights are less frequent and are usually of the kick-and-squeal variety. As two-year-olds most are mated for the first time. They may have changed groups: young fillies, like colts, are intensely explora-tory and they may slip away while the stallion's back is turned. (Another cause for a mare changing groups is that she gets left behind while foaling.) But new group or old, two-year-olds are submissive in any squabbles with adults. It is not until they are three that they are regarded as adults, and even then their behaviour does not settle into adult patterns for another couple of years.

When handled, young horses reflect these social changes in their attitudes. An unhandled two-year-old is far more submissive than a three- or four-year-old, while an older 'wild' horse is more difficult to approach at first but accepts her position better once she is no longer afraid of people.

Teeth Three-year-olds cut their first pair of permanent teeth in spring (well-fed domestic horses do so earlier) and in some the obvious discomfort leads them to eat strange things – mud, stones – or to play with water, splashing openmouthed in it to relieve the hot, swollen palate of lampas.

WHAT DO HORSES DO ALL DAY?

The monumental idleness of the horse. . . .
(E. E. Somerville)

Generally speaking, horses are wonderfully idle and do as little as possible. Most of their time is spent between: eating; dozing or sleeping; and 'loafing', which includes resting and lazy self-comforting behaviour such as standing head to tail swishing flies off each other, stretching, yawning, scratching, rubbing, mutual grooming, rolling, shaking. . . . The more active, dramatic parts of their lives, like fighting, moving from place to place, mating, giving birth, occupy only a small fraction of their time.

Eating

Free-ranging wild horses usually live in relatively poor country now, so it is not surprising that they spend much of their time eating, especially in the winter. They tend to eat in bouts lasting a few hours, followed by a rest. Obviously the length of the bouts depends on how good the food is. What they eat varies a great deal with the time of year and of course the place. Naturally they browse a good deal as well as grazing, taking a wide variety of grasses, rushes (especially in spring), bushes such as gorse or sagebrush, buds and leaves of trees, especially in spring and early summer, acorns (which are poisonous if overeaten) and fruit in autumn, and bark in winter. In some areas they dig up roots of plants, and in snow they paw to reach herbage hidden below.

To lie beside a horse grazing on rough mixed plants and watch her mouth is a revelation. Her wiggly upper lip sorts through plants with impressive efficiency, flipping unwanted leaves aside deftly so that choicer stems and leaves can be snatched. The speed and accuracy of the sorting process, especially in native ponies, can be awe-inspiring when you remember that the horse is not only alert to the barrage of different smells, but also to any strange sight or sound, the position of other ponies in the herd, her distance from her foal, and the flies on her as well as where she is going. The rare mistakes are spat out quickly.

Horses will not eat the lush grass sprouting from places where they have dunged or urinated, not because of the 'sourness' of the grass but because of the smell of their own dung (*see Odberg*). They do relish the patches growing from old cowpats, though, and cows return the compliment. Poisonous plants are not eaten if there is no shortage of food, but domestic horses do eat some poisonous plants dried in hay, and yew, which is deadly, is taken by hungry horses. Prickly plants like thistles, gorse, holly and roses are eaten (carefully) and fruit is a treat: Welsh ponies browse on blackberries and wild plums, spitting the stones out as neatly as any gourmet. The variety of food taken by wild horses usually exceeds that available to domestic ones, and no doubt accounts for their robust health in extremes of weather and emaciation. Adult horses are suspicious of new foods, and it is difficult to persuade wild horses that oats and bread are food. Young horses are typically more adventurous and will come to eat almost anything except onions. In Arab countries horses are regularly fed on household scraps and cooked meals including meat, and in the cold parts of Asia meat is considered an essential part of a horse's diet: Tibetan post horses are fed on fresh sheep's blood mixed with millet, while hungry Icelandic ponies forage on seaweed and fish offal.

Sleeping

Horses sleep about 7 hours in every 24 and sleeping, like eating, is done in bouts. Horses can doze standing up but they usually lie down for at least one sleeping bout; on average they spend 10 per cent of their time lying down, either flat on their sides or more upright, balanced on the breastbone with their feet tucked underneath them. When they want to rest their heads they balance them on their noses, or rather on the teeth, with their lips drawn back so they do not get bruised on hard ground.

Table 11 *Behaviour patterns shown by stallions, mares and geldings*

Stallions	Mares	Geldings
posturing displays (showing off) in courtship, challenge and play, with elevated movements	static courtship display: showing off much rarer	vary
rearing common in courtship, play and fighting	not common	not common
Flehmen to mare's urine	uncommon	not common, though both sexes show Flehmen to other substances too
neigh with tail-off	without	without
more aggressive threat: biting and 'mouthiness' seen in confinement	more defensive threat	?
dung on dungpiles	no dungpiles, face into dunging area	face outwards from dunging area
mark other horses' dung and urine	do not	do not
herding, 'possessiveness' of mares	none	not usual
paternal behaviour: tolerance of foals	maternal behaviour rejection of strange foals	vary
bolder, more alert, more active, heavier muscle	doze on feet more	?

N.B. Geldings vary in the degree of their non-sexuality. Geldings cut late, or cut 'proud' so that the epididymus of the testis is left to produce some testosterone, often show some stallion-like behaviour. Gypsy horses are often cut proud to obtain the muscle, higher spirit and stamina characteristic of the stallion.

Lying down, especially flat, is a vulnerable position, and most horses leap to their feet as soon as they hear anyone approaching: hence the old myth that they always sleep standing up. But they do need to lie down, as it is only when they are lying flat that they dream. Ruckesbusch, who studied sleep in domestic animals, found that the electrical patterns of brain activity typical of dreaming (rapid eye movement or paradoxical sleep) only occur when horses lie flat, and he found that stalled horses lie flat as much as pastured ones even though they spend much more time dozing as well. There are records of horses that had seen action in the First World War kicking and neighing in their sleep, but fortunately most of them dream more peacefully. Foals and youngsters sleep flat more often than adult horses, and foals rarely doze on their feet for long unless they are sick. Horses lie down much less when they are ill (unless rolling with colic, for instance) as if aware that they cannot get up again quickly. When they get up from a good sleep they often stretch, arching their necks, flexing their backs, and stretching each back leg out in turn with the toe neatly turned up.

Loafing

Loafing tends to occupy much of the daytime in the summer, unless it is cool enough for eating. Special places are used for loafing: grouped under a clump of trees, or in a patch of shade, bands of horses while away the hot summer afternoons lazily grooming each other, standing with their heads over their friends' backs, or head to tail swishing the flies off each other ... not exactly dozing but not exactly wide awake either. In hilly country they like to loaf in high, exposed places where a breeze coming up from below keeps the flies away and a broad, open view allows the look-out to spot dangers a good way off. Such places feel secure to a horse. In winter they choose more sheltered spots, backing up under a windbreak. Where horses are kept in large areas you can soon get to know which loafing place they will be in from the weather conditions: there will be hot-weather spots, east wind spots, and so on.

RHYTHMS?

There is no fixed rhythm or routine in the time that these activities follow each other. It is true that when the weather is stable horses tend to do the same things at about the same times. Schafer, whose careful and sympa-

Plate 26 *Group of Arab mares shading their faces from flies under each other's tails as they loaf on a hot summer afternoon in attitudes of complete relaxation. The collar on the nearest one is her identity tag. Al-Marah stud, Tucson.*

thetic observations of horse behaviour show his deep understanding of their 'language', found that his Fjord ponies in Germany tended to feed in the following pattern: 4 or 5 a.m.–7.30 a.m., 11–12 a.m., 3–4 p.m., 5 p.m.– midnight, which is one often adopted in fair weather when it is not too hot. Tyler's New Forest ponies fed all the daylight hours except hot summer afternoons. But the 'rhythm' does not seem to be a routine: it is a flexible, easy-going cycle dictated by weather conditions, or even by whim. This is further shown by psychologist Moyra Williams' observations on stabled horses which, despite being fed at the same time and housed in the same, unvarying stable, showed no routine at all in their cycle of nightly activity.

Why, then, is it a rule in stable management to state that feeding and other activities should follow a strict routine? Mainly it seems to be because, like most other animals, horses do have a kind of internal clock that tells them roughly what time of day it is. If a routine is set up and stuck to strictly, the clock then 'learns' that routine, and the animal's cycle of activity becomes precisely timed. Any little timing mistake, any break in the routine, is then noticed immediately and upsets the animal. Yet it is the training that causes the basis for the upset.

The same is true of people. Those of us who eat meals at strictly regular times find it difficult, and even upsetting, to eat at others; people who wake up at the same time every morning find it difficult to make up for a late night. Those who lead irregular lives without routine suffer far less, for nothing out of the ordinary has happened.

Some animals do have incredibly accurate 'internal clocks' which continue to keep them doing the same thing at the same time even when they are kept in the dark for months on end. We do not, nor do horses, although we do have vague cycles of activity: we are both lackadaisical about time, knowing only roughly whether it is early or late afternoon unless we have put a good deal of effort into training ourselves. Horses that are fed according to the natural pattern, in several feeds spaced evenly throughout the 24 hours without too much regard for times, not only thrive but also suffer less ill-effect from odd days spent hunting, showing or competing.

It may well be that the constant stress of confinement and unnatural feeding is what causes horses to have such delicate stomachs anyway. Pastured horses never spend a whole twelve hours without eating; they eat a good deal more roughage; and they eat a good deal of extremely low quality food without suffering any ill-effect. A recent German computer analysis of over 1000 cases of colic showed that the highest incidences were associated not with feeding but with changes in the weather, which would not upset an 'outside' horse either. This is perhaps an indication that in the conditions of chronic stress produced by unnatural feeding and keeping, any extra little problem is enough to tip the balance and plunge the horse into digestive disorders. Again, veterinarians in America are finding that the stress of sudden confinement in foals can cause perforating ulcers and death. Since horses do not naturally show routines in their behaviour, we should then look to chronic stress as a cause of colic and upset, rather than breaks in routine as such. Again, more facts and figures are needed.

KEEPING IN TRIM: OTHER MAINTENANCE BEHAVIOUR

Drinking

The close-lipped sucking of a horse is an ideal drinking method for an animal which naturally drinks at muddy water-holes, for unlike a dog a horse can filter off the clear top layer without disturbing the rest.

Wild horses drink less often than might be supposed: Przewalski's horses only drink every two or three days, and wild horses in Montana are found grazing as much as ten miles from water, to which they travel only once every day or two (this includes nursing mothers). At a waterhole the stallion drinks first, although he is usually the last to arrive. Waterholes are dangerous places, good hunting for lurking lions, and horses often raise their heads while drinking to gaze around them. Even domestic horses do it. This has been used as a measurement of 'nervousness' in wild horses (*see page 105*).

Typically the hot-blooded breeds drink far less than the cold-blooded; doubtless this is a reflection of the different survival pressures on their ancestors.

Dunging

Horses at grass dung every three to four hours or so. Mares are fairly careless about where they dung but some, especially blood horses, go to areas of rank, previously dunged grass which they face while dunging, so that the area gradually grows larger. Geldings stand within these areas to dung, so that they do not spread. But stallions are most particular about where they dung, and it has a special significance for them.

Many animals have distinct territories which they defend, and many of them scent-mark the boundaries, often with dung or urine, to warn off trespassers.

Although most horses do not defend their territories, and indeed most of them have overlapping ranges, they do have a kind of marking system. Stallions dung in piles, and whenever they come across a dungpile they carefully add their bit on top, like dogs urinating on car wheels. A stallion discovering, or returning to, a dungpile sniffs it with deep concentration and then, with a deal of flourish and braggadocio, steps over it with high, exaggerated paces to line himself up solemnly and add his contribution. Usually he turns round to smell the pile again afterwards, as if to satisfy himself that he has done it right.

When he discovers a mare's dung the stallion urinates on it, often showing Flehmen at the same time. Sometimes he urinates on mare's urine too. In this way the stallion leaves his mark, his scented signature, over the top of everyone else's within his range.

A stallion kept alone in a field also makes dungpiles, and most stabled stallions dung only in one place if the dung is left there, keeping the rest of the box clean. A few geldings dung like stallions, so it is worth trying to encourage this tidy habit in them too.

Figure 25 *Stallion dunging on stallion's dung.*

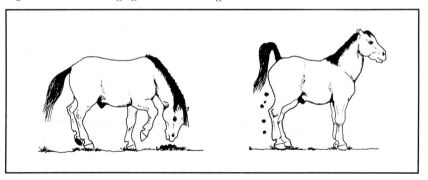

Figure 26 *Stallion urinating on mare's dung.*

Urination

Mares and geldings do not urinate in particular places, nor do stallions
when there is nothing particular to urinate on, but they do tend to come
into a box of fresh bedding and urinate on it apparently deliberately.
Horses' interest in other horses' dung and urine suggest that both carry a
message as to the identity of the horse that did them, and might be used as
such in ways that we do not yet fully understand.

Grooming and self-comforting

Wild horses usually carry a fair number of external parasites (lice and ticks)
as well as internal ones, so their grooming and self-comforting behaviour
is particularly important to them. As well as scratching anywhere they can
reach with their mouths and feet, they rub the bits they cannot reach –
withers, neck, shoulders, rump and tail – on convenient trees or rocks
which may become worn smooth with use. A horse scratching his mouth
and withers shows strange mouth and jaw movements which become

Plate 27 *Two Highland pony friends scratching each other's rumps in the pleasures of mutual grooming. Notice their submissive ears despite the fact that they are actually biting each other: there is no aggression here.* (Photo: Dr T. Clutton-Brock)

biting and scratching when another horse presents itself, and which form the basis for the great ritual of mutual grooming.

'You scratch my back and I'll scratch yours': it is a little ceremony of closeness and mutual help. When one horse approaches another wanting to scratch, she will often open her mouth slightly so that the lower teeth can be seen. Friends begin a mutual grooming bout straight away; strangers too may start grooming after they have carefully sniffed each other's noses, backs and tails without either of them objecting. Most bouts (90 per cent) last less than 3 minutes; some go on for as long as 10 (*Kiley, Feist*). Usually it is the withers that are scratched, but the top of the tail may also be groomed. Both are areas where lice are particularly bad.

Horses have only a limited number of grooming partners, either their family and friends or, if they have none, the horses that stay closest to them in the group. Mutual grooming helps to forge and maintain group links and is a token of confidence and friendship, like the sharing of food in some Plains Indian tribes.

Many horses will scratch a person's back if invited. They are surprisingly

rough, and the rougher you are the more ecstatic they get. This can be used in taming and breaking: once a wild or unhandled horse accepts you scratching her wither and tail she has stopped thinking of you as a danger and takes a much more positive attitude to, and interest in, your later actions.

Rolling

Horses prefer to roll in dusty places or in water, and there are particular favourite rolling places within their range (*see page 126*). A lively and supple horse rolls right over several times, and among older horsemen and gypsies this is regarded as a particularly good sign of vigour. Older and stiffer horses tend to roll on one side first, then get up before repeating the performance on the other side.

Among wild horses different bands use the same rolling spots, and this is seen in domestic horses too. The leading mare rolls first and the stallion last: his scent is thus the first to greet any new band. Sand and snow are also favourite stuff to roll in, and stabled horses often roll in new bedding. Again, this infects the bed with their own scent.

Figure 27 *Rolling and scratching.*

Before rolling a horse sniffs the ground, often paws at it, wiggles his nose in the dust and shakes his tail. He goes down (upper left) by bending his hocks slightly, then collapsing his knees so that his forequarter goes down just before his hindquarter. Rolling on his side (middle left) he rubs his wither well into the dust; if he can manage it he will also squirm about while balanced on his spine (middle right) so that the poll, crest of the neck and tail are scratched too. The horse on the lower left is about to get up but is first scratching his bottom on a convenient rock (note his nose). Getting up (lower right), like going down, is done front end first (cows and horned grasseaters do both the other way round) and requires a strong thrust of the hindquarters to heave the weight on to the front legs; a horse that cannot make this effort may have damaged his back or hips. After a roll, most horses shake vigorously.

Rolling scratches the poll, crest, withers, shoulders, rump and tail, all of which are areas of louse infestation. It also loosens the hair under the saddle and restores circulation after riding. Other main areas of louse infestation are the lower side of the neck and the chest, both of which may be scratched against fences or trees.

Other itchy areas can be reached by the mouth. The yearling (upper right) is reaching to his rear fetlock, a favourite place for ticks, harvest mites (heel bug) and grease. A young horse scratches behind his ears with his back foot (hence the danger of leaving a sturdy headcollar on a youngster) but older horses are less likely to do so.

Attacks by flies

Such attacks are warded off in a number of ways:

by twitching the skin, especially on the shoulders, flanks and back;

by stamping;

by lashing the tail;

by head jerks;

by biting and scratching;

by standing head to tail with a friend, or even just with the head under another horse's tail;

by running into low branches so that the leaves swipe the flies away.

The area behind the girth is a favourite spot for flies to attack, since the skin is particularly thin there. Ridden horses in the summer often turn to bite at flies there and are accused of attacking their riders' feet. Often a flapping trouserleg will tickle this spot, causing intense irritation in a thin-skinned horse.

PLAY

Nothing is more common than for animals to take pleasure in practising whatever instinct they follow at other times for some real good.

(Charles Darwin)

Although the programmes for life-support behaviour are innate and in-herited like the basic body-pattern, they are by no means perfect. Watch a young foal nibbling at grass: she seems to have the right idea, but it is all a little strange and needs polish before it can really be called eating. Watch her experiments at drinking: she lowers her head too far and ends up spluttering with a noseful of water, or tries to peer at it at the same time, or, muddled, thinks that the nibbling programme might work with this stuff too. After a few days' practice, however, she will drink with drooped ears and nostrils wrinkled delicately out of the way like all horses do.

Other behaviour patterns need practising too. Startles, escapes, gallops, explorations, friendships and social behaviour must be practised, and prac-tised well, for a horse's skill in them will affect the quality, and the length, of the rest of his life. And so young horses play.

At first, young foals play mostly with and around their mothers, whose warnings and teaching show them what to avoid at a time when they have no experience. A mare, sensing her young foal straying, will raise her head and watch him before calling him back from danger. She allows him to play around and on her with great tolerance, suffering her tail to be nibbled, her belly to be bumped rudely, and her rest disturbed by his climbing all over her; and she teaches him about mutual grooming. But after a month or so his attentions turn to other foals, and the races, leaps, bucks, forays and friendships begin. Apart from sleeping and eating, most of a foal's time is spent in play, and its importance is shown by the fact that two-thirds of the galloping, and almost all of the fast turns (95 per cent) done by foals are done in play (*Fagen & George*). Play also has enormous importance in learning how to behave in society, for as well as practising their physical coordination, foals are practising their expressions and their skill in understanding signals. They are much more expressive than adult horses, and their nimble grace in pulling faces and waving their tails is excellent practice for later group life. Youngsters that grow up alone, unused to the rough and tumble of group life, are socially as well as physically deprived.

Foals tend to play with others of the same sex, foreshadowing the harem/bachelor groups characteristic of later life. Both sexes enjoy racing, but as time goes on the colts are definitely livelier and more rowdy than the fillies (in New Forest ponies, 50 per cent of all play was between colts, 34 per cent between colts and fillies, and only 16 per cent between fillies). Colts' play-fights, which show all the elements of adult stallion fights, start to get a little too serious, like those of adolescent boys. From an early age they show playful versions of mounting, first on their mothers and later on their playmates. They start chasing and herding too, and will herd and even stamp on sheep and dogs. Fillies play less, and show more of the nibbling that turns quickly to mutual grooming.

Foals and yearlings sometimes approach adult horses to nibble, bite, mount or romp around them. Generally the stallions treat them with tolerance, but a threat signal from an irritable mare sends the youngsters scuttling off 'mouthing' their submission. Stallions especially seem to arouse foals' interest and in wild horse bands the stallions are patient and careful in their play, even with two-year-old colts, but domestic stallions occasionally stamp on and kill young foals. This is doubtless because of the deprived social upbringing of many such stallions.

In youngsters the positive aspects of leadership can be seen clearly. The ringleader is the bold one, the one that goes to investigate anything new, the most cheeky, daring and playful one – and the others follow him. It is leadership rather than aggression that makes a horse important in a group, and nowhere is this seen more plainly than in the attitude of a bright, bold and confident colt.

Adult wild horses do not really play, though windy spring weather may make them active when on the move. But domestic horses, free from the grinding pressures of parasites and inadequate food, often find themselves with excess energy and enjoy a good romp around their field. Sometimes these games get out of hand, as when a good gallop turns into a real stampede and the horses, ancient flight patterns reactivated, seem unable to stop themselves running. Horses kept confined usually play delightedly when first released, and this serves as a good outlet for energy that may otherwise turn into explosive 'games' that a rider may not appreciate. Watching horses at play, either by themselves or with their friends, can give valuable clues to their character, for they play in different ways. One horse gallops freely forward, neck outstretched; another feints and dodges, spooking at shadows; another imagines a lion at her heels, while others pull back and rear, or buck like broncs. All these are natural expressions of those horses' attitudes to life, which are bound to emerge when they are being ridden or driven.

Confined horses often invent little games for themselves in the stable, playing with water, bedding or haynets, but discontented and frustrated horses tend to turn to the classic stable 'vices' instead.

Plates 28 and 29 *Group of yearling Arabs learning social behaviour through games, high-tailing in the excitement of playing follow-my-leader. Champagne leads the line confidently enough, but Colors on Parade (second) humps his back at Royal Riven to warn him not to come too close (note one ear towards the photographer, one towards Riven). As Royal Riven checks himself his ears go back into a submissive position. Typically, only the leader has his ears pricked; both Grenelefe (fourth) and Beverly Bloom (fifth) are flicking theirs about.*
Colors on Parade giving trouble again, this time threatening Beverly Bloom. Colors threatens with his ears as well as his body, cutting off Beverly Bloom's path. The other yearlings (left to right) Grenelefe, Champagne and Royal Riven, are all taking note of the rumpus. Although Colors on Parade is the most aggressive of the group he is by no means the leader: in fact, his behaviour is helping to break the group up rather than draw it together. Such games are excellent practice in social behaviour: youngsters that grow up alone, deprived of this practice, are slow to respond to other horses' signals and are liable to have difficulty when mating. Al-Marah stud, Tucson.
(Photos: Louise Serpa)

Figure 28 *Play moves in frisky adult horses. Although these two horses (Bill on the left, Chloe on the right) both leap and buck, they do so in characteristically different ways. Bill moves squarely, in an honest fashion which is typical of his whole personality, while Chloe's uncoordinated, twisted leaps reveal her characteristic quirkiness.*

All these everyday activities show three characteristics:

(a) They are group activities.
(b) They are affected by the weather.
(c) They tend to happen in particular places.

Infectious behaviour

Social animals living in groups tend to do the same things at the same time. On the whole they do not behave as a hotch-potch of different individuals each doing a different thing, but as a unit. Shoals of fish turn in unison, flocks of birds wheel in formation, and other people infect us with their moods, their latest catchphrases, and their yawns. For a social animal, behaviour is infectious.

Horses are no exception. They eat as a group, drink as a group, rest, roll, loaf and move off as a group. A change of programme spreads like a virus through them. Of course they are not like a regiment, for the point of being in a group would be lost if they were. Not all the group can sleep at the same time, for who would then keep watch? In fact, wild horses never sleep, or eat, all at the same time. There are always one or two on their feet, watching, taking their turn as guardians of the group. Stallions, temperamentally more alert than brood mares, tend to do more watching than the rest. When one stops watching and drifts off to sleep one of the others, full enough or rested enough, starts to feel uneasy and becomes the watcher. As for the rest, they copy each other.

This natural copying means that horses, especially bored ones, tend to pick up habits from each other. In one stable yard they may go in for chewing the woodwork of their stalls; in another weaving may be the latest fashion. Stable habits and stable vices, which have their roots in

Figure 29 *Habits can be infectious too. Tongue-lolling is usually seen in horses that are not comfortable with the bit (often a straight curb). However, other horses do it when free, apparently when they are feeling doubtful or uncertain. It is not a common habit. This particular horse was a tongue-loller when he arrived in a large stud farm for breaking. Within a couple of months many of the horses there, particularly the young ones, would stick their tongues out whenever they were hesitant or doubtful, so that strangers visiting the youngsters were greeted by an array of dubious faces and waving tongues. Fortunately none of the horses that developed this odd habit did it when wearing a bit, although many of them later started to enjoy wiping their lolling tongues against the metal bars of their gates. Some horses stick their tongues straight out and appear to enjoy having them stroked, though this does not seem to be catching.*

boredom and frustration, find their expression in a number of different modes whose particular form often originates in copying the horse next door.

But the horse's talent for being infected ('social facilitation') can be extremely useful to the unselfconscious trainer, once he has the horse's attention. Slow, calm movements tend to calm horses, while a quick charade of friskiness will encourage them to play. Showing off can be encouraged by grandiose flourishes, waving and running; short, loud, toneless whistles encourage snorting, and, strange as it may sound, one of the ways of enticing a suspicious horse to take new food is to pretend to eat it yourself. Again, these techniques depend on the fact that horses transfer their social feelings to us: we claim their attention, and are trustworthy, and so worthwhile copying.

Weather

Horses are immensely sensitive to weather. To stay in good condition they must eat, sleep and drink a certain amount every day, but the time they choose to do these activities depends on the weather. They eat more or less continuously until their small stomachs are full, unless unpleasant degrees of sun, rain or wind prevent them.

Cold weather does not particularly bother them if it is dry, and a period of high pressure in the winter, bringing acute cold and clear skies, makes them bright and frisky. *Rain* is hated, though usually not enough to bring them inside. Unless the rain is prolonged they stop eating and stand with their backs to the wind behind a windbreak, tails flat, backs hunched, heads low. They get cold soon when they are wet, and shiver violently. *Strong winds* are also disliked, and may make horses very irritable. Horses shelter against them as against rain, always turning their backs to the wind. *Light winds* and *gusty breezes*, on the other hand, tend to make them skittish and playful: 'getting the wind up his tail' may be the prelude to running away or bucking, for in a wind the horse flattens his tail, hunching his back and bringing his hocks under him so that he is perfectly positioned for sudden bursts of energy. Gusts of wind may cause a horse to skip sideways, head turned away, as if he were dancing with it. *Thundery weather*, that electric prelude to a storm, makes them jumpy and restless, tense and wary; stabled horses, in particular, may become very agitated before and during storms, perhaps because all their natural feelings tell them that they should be somewhere else. Their coats accumulate static electricity in hot or thundery weather, and fast stroking with the flat of the hand may produce a firework display of crackles and sparks which may be strong enough to jerk or hurt your hands: it must be strange to be enclosed in a coat charged up like that.

Heat makes horses lethargic, and on hot summer afternoons they look for shade. The changing breezes of dawn and dusk make them lively and playful. On the whole their spirits, like those of many people, rise and fall with the barometer, though they dislike heat, and like cold, more than we do.

Ridden horses turn their heads sideways or lower them against rain, whisk round to turn their backs to a strong wind if possible, and hunch their backs when cold too. When breaking and training it is worth while remembering that weather affects horses more than us.

SPACE AND DISTANCE

Most animals, ourselves included, have a strong sense that the space immediately around them belongs to them. Herring gulls perched on a cliff space themselves at regular intervals, and do not allow others to intrude into their personal space; trout rank themselves evenly across a stream; horses sheltering under a windbreak space themselves at a comfortable distance from each other. Our own personal space extends further in front of us than behind or to the side: in a crowded room we feel fairly comfortable back to back or alongside strangers, but cannot tolerate them at the same distance immediately in front of us. It is as if we had an invisible bubble around us, into which only intimate companions – lovers, family, close friends – are allowed. This is called *individual distance*.

A horse's individual distance, some six to ten feet, extends further in front and behind than to the sides. This is partly due to the structure of the eye. As with ourselves, only intimates – friends, a foal – are allowed within that distance except in meetings, when horses want to identify each other by smell, or in mating. When they meet, strange horses hesitate as the outsides of their invisible bubbles touch, watching for signs of an invitation to go forward. A horse that invades another's personal space without this invitation, as playing foals are likely to do, is driven out: the personal space is defended. It seems that the individual distance of an aggressive bully is greater than that of a submissive animal. This is partly why they threaten and attack other horses so much, for they feel 'invaded' when other horses merely feel comfortably close.

Plate 30 *Welsh mountain ponies, grazing in a group despite the vast area they could spread out over, are careful to keep their individual distance from each other. The only one within another pony's personal space is the foal peeking over his mother's neck.*

Figure 30 *The horse's idea of space.* Left: *the inner ring represents the horse's individual space inside which he does not want another horse unless he has invited it. If another horse invades this space, he will either threaten him so that he moves away or move away himself, depending on how aggressive a character he is. The outer ring represents his flight distance. If any strange animal, particularly a threatening one, comes within this distance the horse will run away.* Right: *two horses loafing side by side keep their individual distance from each other unless they are keeping the flies off each other, or are close friends or relations.*

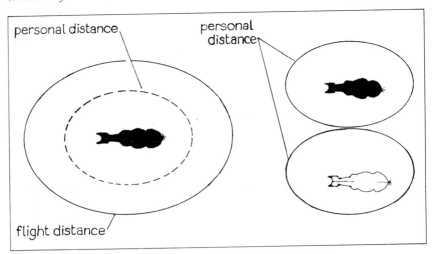

Thoroughly domesticated horses are quite used to people barging into their personal space, but partially-handled ones, or loose horses, recognize a line over which they do not want you to step unless invited. One way that they invite you is to move towards you as you hesitate politely outside their bubble, but there are subtler ways of inviting too, and often the mere lack of threat or nervousness can be taken as an invitation. Nevertheless imitating the horse's way of hesitating politely is a wise move, for a forced intrusion is grounds for defensive attack or flight.

Many domestic stallions seem not just to tolerate but positively to like people within their space, and step forward boldly to stand with the shoulder almost, but not quite, touching you. This is exactly the position occupied by the mare's rump just before the stallion mounts her, and so has a pleasurably sensual flavour for him; but for most people it is an intrusion on *their* personal space, and so is alarming.

Flight distance is the larger distance that horses keep between themselves and anything that may be threatening, especially predators. It extends farther to the back than to the front. A startled horse will dash to the limit of this distance before wheeling to face the danger. Its boundaries vary according to the threat: thus there are distances at which you or a predator are allowed to pass by with your head down, your attention elsewhere, but if you turn to look directly at them the horses will move away. It is as if our personal space is seen as extending further in front of us than to our sides, and if that extension invades the horse's flight distance then the horse will move away. This can be used in gaining the confidence of hesitant, unhandled horses, which are far more likely to approach you if you do not look directly at them, and if you crouch to reduce your space.

Herd distance Although they do not like to be too close together, horses do not like to be outside a certain distance from each other either. This distance varies enormously between individuals, and also according to circumstances: thus frightened horses clump together much more than confident, secure ones.

HOME RANGES, TERRITORIES, MAPS AND HOMING

Horses have a great sense of, and memory for, places and directions. This is important to them in their natural life, not merely for finding food and water but also because they need to know where to run in an emergency: once they are galloping they can not see well.

Home ranges

Wild horse home ranges, like their band sizes, vary according to what kind of land they cover (*see page 52*). (Here 'home range' is used to mean the area that the horses wander over, while 'territory' is used only when that area is defended against other bands.) Only rarely do stallions defend their territories; in most cases the home ranges of several bands overlap. Most stallions defend only their harems, challenging strange stallions who come near although unlike truly territorial animals they are not arguing about ownership of a particular place.

The relics of this 'home range' instinct are seen in domestic horses which, when turned out on new pasture, walk the fence. Once they have accepted an area as their home range horses will often stay within it despite sagging fences or gates left open, for if the pasture is adequate there is no pressing reason to escape. Stabled horses whose lack of experience, or bad experiences, have taught them that the outside world is a fearful and traumatic place, may even become unwilling to leave their protected sanctuaries, although a healthy-minded horse that is enjoying his work is unwilling to go back inside unless he knows there is food there.

Spots

Within their ranges horses reserve particular spots for particular activities. No matter how small the area, be it only a few square yards of stable, there are not only favourite eating places but also favourite loafing spots, sleeping areas, rolling spots, dunging areas, and so on. Often the reasons behind their choosing those particular spots are beyond us, but they are not working on force of habit alone: there are generally good reasons, obvious to any horse, why one place is preferable to another. To stand in one of these spots and begin to savour the reasons is to begin to sense what it is like to be, and to perceive like, a horse. Loafing spots, for example, have not only a certain amount of weather and fly protection but also good views or good escape routes. Since the relative values of these factors change with the weather, it is not surprising that there may be several different spots used in different circumstances.

Wild horses roam over large areas, and one of their special learning talents is for remembering where certain things happened. Domestic horses also have this talent, often more markedly than their owners, and often show signs of remembering some fearful, painful or delightful event that the rider has forgotten or not noticed. Such superb feats of memory are, sadly, usually unappreciated or even punished as silliness. Arabs, particularly easily startled, are also good at remembering black spots where frights occurred. Memories of these single events may persist for years even if the spots are not revisited.

Plate 31 *Monarch of all he surveys: given the freedom to wander over this whole valley and two mountains, Maestoso chooses this high rocky knoll as his favourite loafing spot. Exposed places feel safe to a horse: he likes the sense of security in being able to see all around him, although in bad weather he will go to a more sheltered spot that still offers a view of approaching tigers.*

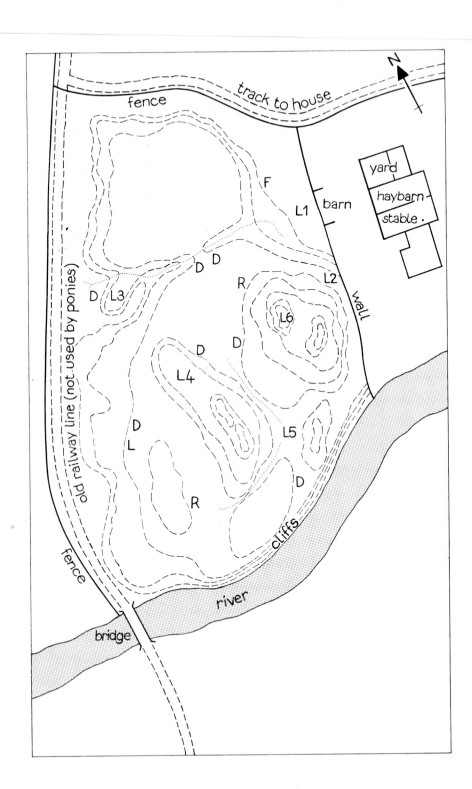

Maps

A horse's mental maps are based not only on highlights and black spots or, as some would put it, on positive or negative reinforcement. Their ability to make mental maps of an area independently of goals or rewards is far greater than our own, which is perhaps why we fail to understand it or to give them credit for it. Many animals have this ability. Kavanau, a student of mouse behaviour, built a maze that consisted of 427 metres of runway. In it there were 1205 right-angle turns and 445 blind alleys, whose openings made up half the total choices. Yet when he put wild white-footed Californian mice in it he found that after only two or three days the mice could run from one end to the other faultlessly despite the fact that until the time of testing they had had no reward or punishment. They had simply remembered from their explorations. 'It is unlikely,' he said, 'that these remarkable learning performances even begin to approach the capacities of these animals.' One cannot imagine human beings beginning to

Figure 31 *Sketch map of area used by ponies (November).*

This enclosure is used by two young mares at a riding school. It is a craggy hill, bristling with outcrops of granite, rising from the flat fields of a reclaimed estuary. The flat strip on the west provides good grazing, while on the higher land patches of grass are interspersed with patches of bracken and gorse. Among the crags scrub oak, a few mountain ash, some holly and birch grow. The ponies browse new growth of holly and gorse, and in November had entirely stripped the bark of two fallen mountain ash.

Prevailing winds are from the west; in the winter snow comes from the north, and biting cold winds from the east. Sixteen other horses are kept in groups on the fields to the north, west and south, while daily activity centres round the hay barn and stable. The mares (cob X Lipizzan) are in excellent condition and very hardy. Contour lines (drawn by eye) at approximately 25-foot intervals.

F: hay dropped here in winter

D: areas of greatest dunging

R: noted rolling spots, amongst crushed bracken

L: loafing spots (note that none of these is on the low ground)

L_1: muddy area used when waiting for food. The pair also shelter from rain against the barn

L_2: favoured spot on a rise amongst trees: good view of the barn and stable, view of the house and track (and food-bringers) and protection from the west

L_3: a flat plateau overlooking the fields to the west, well protected from the east and north

L_4: a higher plateau with clear views over the north, west and south

L_5: protected spot with views to south

L_6: the top of the world, a favourite good-weather spot that requires a scramble to reach

approach them either. Sadly, no similar studies have been made on horses, whose map-making abilities are often shown under less controlled conditions. Two facts are worth mentioning: first, the mice were used to following their own decisions and not those of 'handlers'; and second, other studies of animals' learning abilities show that domestic animals, kept in dull, deprived environments compared to the rich world of the wild, are unlikely to develop these learning capacities to the full. Without the opportunity they cannot learn how to learn. Nevertheless it would be interesting to know what were the map-making abilities of any horses.

Skinner's learning theory (*see page 42*) fails to explain this type of rewardless learning, at which horses are particularly good.

Homing

As well as being able to recognize paths and places, horses can find their way home over strange country. We do not know whether they use true compass-type direction-finding like those real wizards of homing, pigeons and salmon for instance, or whether they do it by mental maps and recognizing landmarks. In Moyra Williams' brief study, her horses tended to go upwind rather than in the right direction in totally strange country, and even relatively close to home they lost direction when they had to go downwind without landmarks. When they were trailered several miles from home they tried to return home rather than to their trailer. Again, there is a sad lack of horses that have had any practice at homing, and a sad lack of more extensive study.

Allowing a horse to 'home' from a place he has not been before is a fascinating exercise, for it allows us to appreciate what cues are important to a horse in his normal wanderings. When turning back after a long ride out into strange country they often use smell at junctions of paths, sniffing each one intently before setting off briskly on the right one. Whether they are smelling their own hoofprints, or remembering smells they registered on the way out, is not known. When they take a 'wrong' path it usually turns out to be a short-cut back to the right one, though whether they are using landmarks or sense of direction is again not known. Whatever they are using, they are better at homing than we are, as many a lost and tired huntsman or horseman has had good reason to appreciate.

Exploration

An Elephant's Child – who was full of 'satiable curiosity.
(Rudyard Kipling)

In free-ranging animals exploration is particularly important, and inquisitiveness about anything new is one of the horse's chief characteristics. Young horses especially are almost insatiably curious.

For a foal there is an enormous amount to discover about the world, and a number of ways of finding out: by smelling, listening and watching, by tasting, licking and chewing, by pawing (foals paw at strange things far more than do adult horses, who tend to paw in frustration rather than investigation), and by exploring round strange corners. At first a foal does not explore far from his mother but later he grows bolder, though still as it were attached to her by an invisible elastic that pulls him back to her whenever fear overtakes him. When he finds some curious new object a young horse will peer at it intently, stretching out his tense, arched neck until his nose touches it; bumping his nose often gives him enough of a shock to make him pull back and start again with his smelling, testing and chewing investigations.

Plate 32 *Mustang colt out on a solitary exploration through the desert. He is highly alert, his tight mouth, tensely kinked tail and snappy action showing his conflict between the excitement of exploring and his natural caution. Arizona.*

As yearlings, colts are noticeably bolder than fillies and as two-year-olds both explore still further. In wild horses this leads to their setting off with their friends on forays that may lead them to switch bands. Youngsters that have been brought up in confinement also take great pleasure in excursions into the wide world. Encouraging this exploratory drive pays full dividends later on, for it produces a horse that approaches the world boldly and with delight rather than fear and anxiety. It seems that the second and third years of a horse's life are some kind of critical period in the development of this attitude. This no doubt has its origins in the natural changes that take place as a wild horse grows up. During this time foals must become independent of their mothers, and if they are colts they later become independent of the parent band too. Driven out by the stallion, these colts must cope with the strain of finding new ground and perhaps mares of their own. In fact it does not seem a strain, rather a huge and enjoyable game. But domestic horses, deprived of the chance of developing their exploratory instincts until after they are broken in protected circumstances as three-year-olds, become as nervous as overprotected children: they do not take easily to the overwhelming number of new sensations that they meet when they first go out, and their fearful attitude often involves them in accidents and unpleasantnesses that simply convince them that the world is a frightening and painful place.

MEETING

On these explorations, horses are bound to meet each other. What happens when they do?

Being social animals, horses are intensely interested in each other. At first glimpse they usually want to investigate each other more closely. When two wild horse bands meet, each stallion quickly makes sure that his band is in order before stepping forward to challenge the other, often snorting loudly and swelling his muscles in an impressive display. The proud posturing and prancing that follow may be enough to make a submissive stallion remove himself and his harem. If the challenge is taken up, though, it usually leads to a *dungpile ritual*: the two stallions, circling each other warily though still displaying mightily, find the nearest dung-pile where each in turn makes a grand display of dunging and sniffing. Again there is plenty of opportunity for the one that is outfaced to move away without damage or fighting, but if neither submits by moving away (leaving the 'winner' to make sure that the last bit of dung on the pile is his) then a fight may develop. On the whole, though, if the contest can be won by display and flourish alone then fighting is avoided.

The dungpile ritual is very similar to the urinating ritual that two male dogs often go through when they meet, and again the same signals of noise, swelling to appear larger, exaggerated movements and scent-marking are used.

When other horses meet they hesitate a few yards from each other as their personal spaces touch before deciding for or against a closer encounter. Usually a nursing mare refuses to allow a stranger nearer, driving the other away with threat or moving away herself and calling her foal to her. But if the signals are right then the two strangers move in, sniffing carefully

Plate 33 *Tremendous excitement evident in this highly charged meeting between two colts. Beaming Sun (left) shows characteristic tension in his stiff neck, with a tight mouth, wild eyes and mane, and flickering ears revealing that he barely knows what he is going to do next. Wild Bill, altogether a calmer and more well-balanced character, arches his neck and concentrates on sniffing from a distance. Beaming Sun's attitude made this meeting explode into a prolonged and rowdy play-fight.*

at each other's nostrils with enormous interest. Usually they do not face each other directly but stand at an angle, for during the huge exchange of signals that follow – the flickering ears that show emotional changes, the nickers and squeals that welcome or warn, and the constant stream of smell-information whose subtlety and importance we cannot even guess at – one possible move is a lightning foreleg strike that can cripple a knee. At some point one horse may try to drive the other away with threats, and a mare that is not in season will resist a hopeful stallion with indignant squeals and kicks. But if the meeting is peaceful and pleasurable the pair go on blowing and sniffing, moving on to sniff at shoulders, flanks, rumps and genitals; the whole affair may even lead to a bout of mutual grooming, embarked on tentatively. Age, sex and group differences, as well as each horse's emotional position at the time (Is she lonely? Is she an intruder on another mare's field? another gelding's field? Is she lost, or out looking for a stallion?) mean that there are a vast number of possible outcomes to these meetings, and a different set of pressures on each one. The mutual decision that the horses arrive at is based on an incredibly delicate and accurate information exchange whose swift signals are fascinating to watch. (Appendix 1 gives accounts of a number of such meetings and the animals' reactions.)

Young and wild horses do not know any other way to investigate other animals (including people) and until they have sniffed at your face and hair they seem to feel that they do not know you properly. Where smell establishes identity, ears and voice, and perhaps also the pattern of breaths, establish emotional state: in a meeting with an adult unhandled horse you are at a distinct disadvantage since you do not fully understand the signals you are giving out, and since in many cases you have to crouch before a wild horse will approach you it is safer to remain passive than to try active communication in an unknown 'language'. A foreleg strike from an indignant mare, or a bitten face, might be the result of well-intentioned nose-blowing. But most domestic horses have been discouraged from smelling faces and are content to examine a strange person from a distance, however small. Scratching the withers of a horse is a more natural gesture of unmistakeable friendliness. Even without very close examination horses recognize their human and horse friends by sight and voice, while the many instances of man-hating or (more rarely) woman-hating horses that attack 'on sight' must mean that our smell, or possibly the sexual differences in the way we move, must be stronger than we think.

Ridden horses also want to meet and explore strange horses, but the possibility that one of them might react aggressively can make this alarming for their riders. Stallions, easily recognizable from their cresty necks,

Table 10 *Meetings: questions and answers*

Questions	How investigated	Answers	Possible reactions
It moves, so:			
1 Is it a horse?	sight, voice	no	probably move away unless known friend
		yes	move closer, investigate (2)
2 Friendly?	sight	yes	move closer, investigate (3)
		no	move away
		unwelcome	threaten
		(e.g. to dam of new foal)	
3 Stranger?	sight, smell, voice	yes	move closer, investigate (4)
		no	revert to previous relationship
4 What sex?	sight (display), smell	same	stallions: dungpile ritual
			others: investigate (5)
		opposite	in-season mare and stallion: courtship
			out-of-season mare and stallion: attempted courtship, rejection by mare, herding
			gelding with mare: (5)
			youngsters: (5)
5 Close check: maturity attitude	smell, voice, ears, movements	possible friend	mutual grooming
			play in youngsters
		not interesting	move away
		threatening	defensive threat, move away
		unwelcome	aggressive threat

exaggerated movements and loud voices, are always best kept at a distance since they are liable to become extremely excited and, however well-trained and ridden, difficult to restrain in close meetings with other horses. When ridden in company, a stallion is best kept in the lead lest he upset the other horses by herding them.

RESULTS OF MEETINGS: AGREEMENTS, DISPLAYS AND FIGHTING

Once horses have established each other's identity they have to work out an agreement about how they feel about each other. Usually this is resolved peacefully: friendships may be struck up straight away by lonely horses; youngsters may start playing with each other; or they may agree to ignore each other. In competititive circumstances, as when two harems want to use the same waterhole, there may be a struggle for precedence; and when a newcomer is introduced into an established group she may upset them so that they turn on her with threats. In the relative confinement of a paddock the newcomer cannot escape, and so may vent her feelings of stress on the younger or more submissive members of the group until at last they settle down together. As we have seen (*see page 53*) the relationships between horses in a group are a complex web of likes and dislikes, and the equilibrium of an established group is a balance worked out in space such that all individuals are at what they consider a comfortable distance from their various companions. Dropping a newcomer into this creates disturbances that upset everybody until the web stretches and shifts into a new pattern of equilibrium. In various types of meeting, then, the result may not be peaceful but a clash which is usually resolved by an exchange of signals called a display.

Displays The point of displays – impressive displays, courtship, threat displays, dungpile rituals, and so on – is to achieve mutual agreement through the use of signals. Fighting benefits no one. Threat displays (*see page 82*) come in various strengths, since some opposition takes more scaring away than others. When a horse wishes to attack he uses aggressive threat, but when he feels attacked but either cannot or does not want to submit by moving away he uses defensive threat. In wild horses it is more characteristic of stallions to use aggressive threat, and of mares to use defensive threat, when a serious argument is developing (though an aggressive mare does use aggressive threat at first before turning round if her threats are ignored). A good deal about horses' feelings towards people is shown in the fact that almost all the threats they use towards us are defensive ones: turning away with flattened ears, presenting the rump and threatening to kick are not attacks on us but defences against us. Head thrusts, so commonly used at other horses, are given to people passing by stables but rarely to people in the stable or paddock. On the contrary, when horses feel like attacking us they usually bite 'for real', not in threat, and they tend to do it fast and sneakily, often when our backs are turned.

Fights seem to be rare in wild horses, which tend to use threat displays in battles of will and bravado rather than physical violence. Among horses kept more closely confined minor fights break out more often. Squabbles erupt at feeding times, or between aggressive horses which have run themselves into a corner together. But pitched battles, usually between stallions, do sometimes occur in the wild, and they are frightful.

Battles often start almost without warning, with only minimal threat displays. This tendency is fairly common amongst other animals too: elephants have superb threat displays, but it seems that the more they threaten the less likely they are to attack. Aggressive dogs, too, often fly at each other without bothering to use their threat displays. Fighting stallions charge at each other, rearing up and trying to bite each other's necks, tearing at the huge, poorly protected jugular vein and windpipe. Many aim to get the opponent on the ground, either by pushing him over as both rear up or by biting him behind the elbows, which brings him to his knees as he snatches his foreleg back against the pain. Once grounded, a horse is at a huge disadvantage not only physically but, more important, psychologically. In trying to manœuvre into a good attacking position without becoming vulnerable, the stallions may 'waltz' around each other nose to tail, shoulder-barging as they go. The commonest injuries from these battles are broken jaws and damaged knees, either of which lead to an early death in the wild.

STALLIONS

Stallion behaviour differs from mare behaviour in many ways. Some of these may seem fairly trivial, but others embody completely different attitudes towards other horses and the world in general. In domestic horses,

A

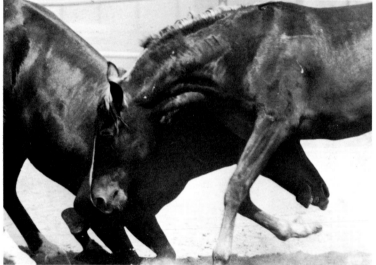

B

C

Plate 34 *Colts' play-fights show all the moves used by stallions in battles. (A) Wild Bill, one foot over Beaming Sun's wither, lunges open-mouthed for the jugular and wind-pipe. (B) Beaming Sun, on his knees after Bill bit him behind the elbow, tries to do the same back to Bill. (C) Waltzing gives room for a breather since, like boxers in a clinch, neither can get at the other. (Drawing) Bill rears up and lunges forward to knock Beaming Sun off his feet.*

Although Wild Bill definitely won on points, Beaming Sun never admitted defeat and turned the fight into a gruelling race. It was his flighty provocation that annoyed the good-tempered Bill in the first place.

stallions are far rarer than mares or geldings, and their different needs may be overlooked, leading to difficulties in handling. Much of their behaviour, even their non-sexual behaviour, is due to the presence of the male sex hormone, testosterone: geldings do not show such behaviour but half-castrated cryptorchids or 'rigs', whose one remaining undescended testis is capable of producing testosterone although not fertile sperm, do behave like stallions. The seasonal variation in testosterone production, which is high in the spring and summer but low in the winter, makes stallions more 'stallionish' in the spring although they may behave like geldings in the winter. Mares with malfunctioning ovaries may have severe hormonal imbalances that lead them to behave like stallions, and when this change happens rapidly the difference in 'character' produced is striking, and clearly bewildering to the mare.

Anabolic steroids, now used to increase muscular development in sports horses (and athletes!) are closely related to testosterone: it is testosterone that promotes the heavier muscling characteristic of stallions, and the use of anabolic steroids to mimic this may also produce degrees of stallion behaviour. One of the characteristic effects of testosterone in other animals is to increase the animal's perseverance or determination at whatever he wants to do; but this has not been tested in horses.

Posturing Stallions are great *poseurs*. A wild stallion seeing another horse steps out high, snorting at the intruder and striking dramatic attitudes. If the other is a stallion, a dungpile ritual (*see page 130*) follows; if she is a mare the stallion moves round her in a proud little dance, displaying himself in 'airs above the ground'. Some of the classical *haut-école* movements are refinements of the stallion's natural posturing dance, tidied up and 'shaped' to give them cued precision without losing their elegance and brilliance. They are not normally seen in mares, which, when they step high in mild alarm or excitement, lack the powerful slow cadence of the stallion's display.

Herding and possessiveness Stallions running with mares herd their harems by running behind them, slightly to one side, with the head and neck outstretched and low. This threatening behaviour keeps the last members of the group together; sometimes the stallion directs them by wheeling out to one side and driving the band away from him, like a dog working sheep. Herding behaviour is not seen in mares and is an expression of the stallion's strong possessiveness. In heavily stocked lush pasture on Shackleford Banks the pony stallions express this feeling still further in true

Table 9 *What horses do all day*

Duncan and Boy watched the herd of feral Camargue ponies at the Tour du Valat field station to determine their 'time-budgets', i.e., the percentage of time spent at each activity. They found the stallions to be more alert and active, and to eat less than the mares.

Spring to Autumn 1976	Standing resting	Lying up	Lying flat	Standing alert	Trotting	Galloping	Rolling	Walking	Eating
Adult mares, foal at foot	20	4	0.6	6.8	0.4	0.2	0.05	9	58.5
Young mares and all yearlings	15	7	2.7	7.2	0.6	0.2	0.1	9.4	57.5
2 – 3-year-old colts	14	8	1.5	10.1	0.4	0.35 ·	0.17	8.5	57.4
Adult stallions	16	5	1.9	11.1	0.5	0.4	0.26	10	55.1
New foals (taken from a different study on same group)	8	18	15	31	1.8	1.8	?	18	13

NB 1. Feist (Pryor Mountain mustangs) found that the stallions rolled more than the mares, and that the lead stallion rolled last (scent significance?).

2. Berger (Grand Canyon horses) counted the number of times a horse raised his head during drinking to calculate an index of nervousness, and found the stallions less nervous than the mares.

3. Ruckebusch, investigating sleep in cows and horses, found that paradoxical sleep (dreaming) happened only in the lying flat position. Paradoxical sleep appears to be concerned with sorting out the impressions and experiences of waking life. It is interesting to see that youngsters sleep flat more than adults, and that stallions, which are generally more alert and active than mares, also sleep flat more than mares do.

Figure 32

His ears up-prick'd; his braided hanging mane
Upon his compass'd crest now stands on end;
His nostrils drink the air, and forth again,
As from a furnace, vapours doth he send:
His eye, which scornfully glisters like fire,
Shows his hot courage and his high desire.
        Shakespeare, Venus and Adonis

No mistaking the challenge in the attitude of this stallion snorting as he steps out to
investigate another stallion. He shows the same characteristics as the courting stallion –
high tail, high, exaggerated steps, and arched neck – but his head is held much more
horizontally.

territorial behaviour, defending their harem territories from intruders; in
the Camargue, in contrast, the stallions allow their harems to mix freely
with those of other stallions, but they do not allow these stallions to pay
attention to 'their' mares.

Watching wild horses in Montana, Feist found that herding behaviour
occurred for the following reasons:

in 40 per cent of cases to drive the mares away from another group or
stallion;

in 30 per cent to direct the group when on the move;

in 12 per cent to single out a mare from the group to court her;

in 12 per cent to drive away non-members of the herd;

in 4 per cent to herd in new members.

A wild stallion running with a harem has a rich social life, mares to possess, freedom, and as much activity and interest as he wants. Psychologically he is well equipped to deal with that kind of life. But a confined stallion, alone in his box, has none of these things: nothing that his behaviour is designed for is there. This mismatch between reality and his expectations (in an evolutionary sense) results in confusion, frustration and all too often aggression, especially in the hot-blooded types. This is naturally expressed more often in biting than in kicking. (Over 80 per cent of stallion fights involve biting and over 75 per cent involve front-leg strikes, but only half show back-leg kicking. When mares fight they threaten to bite just as often as stallions do, but when they start to fight seriously they actually bite much less, turning round to kick instead.) The savage biting and snapping often seen in confined stallions is an expression of frustration turned to aggression.

Unfortunately the stallion's needs and frustrations are often confused with ideas about 'dominance', and it is held that stallions are more 'dominant' and therefore need stronger handling than other horses. Yet stallions submit to aggression from their mares, or to more aggressive horses in their bachelor group, as meekly as other horses, so the question of submission cannot be said to be any harder for them. As we have seen, the idea of dominance is not a particularly helpful one anyway in analysing relationships; but what is important in dealing with a stallion is a proper understanding of his needs. When these needs are dealt with a stallion is as placid and tractable as any other horse.

Running out with mares is ideal for a stallion, and if he has had a proper social upbringing he will hurt neither them nor himself. But the prejudices of mare-owners, who tend to be more impressed by a shiny, hot-tempered beast prancing in a spotless yard than a scruffier and happier fellow loafing in a field, put pressure on the stud-owner to stable the stallion. There are simple ways of alleviating the stresses of even a stabled horse. Lack of exercise is common in stud stallions, which often get a high-protein, high-energy diet to maintain a high level of fertility, and seldom get the chance to burn it off. If a stallion is regularly ridden out in company he soon becomes more placid and happy, for he has enough to exercise both his alert mind and his muscular body; he also becomes less excitable in company. Giving him a stable companion satisfies his possessiveness and his social needs. Good manners (not biting) are part of any horse's education; but many stallions are given so little freedom, and so little chance to satisfy the needs which they cannot help generating, that their frustration reaches a peak where they can barely stop themselves savaging their handlers and their mares. Knowing they will be punished for it unfortunately may make them faster and more dangerous: it is wiser, as well as more humane, to try to eliminate the cause of the problem rather than merely discourage the symptoms – and the cause lies in the conditions in which they are kept.

Stabling It is a curious fact, and one that shows our ignorance of a horse's natural feelings, that stable blocks are usually built facing inwards with walkways directly past the boxes. A stallion in such a box has his desires constantly teased by a procession of delectable bottoms, horse or human, whizzing by and begging to be herded: small wonder that, like a child with candy waved in front of his face, he becomes enraged. Given a large area of varied land a stallion chooses high, exposed vantage points with good views as his loafing spots. A stable with a panoramic view where a visitor can be seen approaching from a distance rather than popping up like a jack-in-the-box is much closer to his natural choice, and more soothing to his senses, than an enclosed yard with its circus of near-range excitements.

A contented stallion, gentle in his strength and brilliant in his pride, is a joy both to watch and to be with.

DEATH

A dying horse, like a foaling mare, often wanders to a damp spot: bogs and ditches attract birth and death. 'Old age' deaths in domestic horses are mostly due to some form of heart failure. Horses seldom die quietly: they kick like shot rabbits even after their hearts have stopped beating, and the signs of their struggles often lead to the supposition that they have had heart attacks while trying to get out of marshy places. It is, of course, difficult to be sure what has happened, but the fact that too many wise old horses that certainly knew better have been found dead in bogs seems to show that some of the deaths are not the accidents they first appear to be. Tyler, for example, mentions that the major cause of death in adult New Forest ponies (none of which was over 18 years) was falling into bogs and ditches; these were ponies that had lived in the same area all their lives. Again, there are too few facts and figures. Many animals, especially herd animals, do appear to know when death is near and move away from the herd for the event; perhaps water smells particularly attractive at that time.

Horses take remarkably little notice of death or dead horses, even their friends, but mares with foals that have died sometimes stay with the corpses for days, refusing to rejoin their harems. But when the foal has died at birth the mare does not appear to miss it: she needs to see, hear and smell it alive, or to feed it, before her full maternal feelings are released.

Horses are seldom afraid of fresh blood, despite the old sayings, but the reek of stale blood from an abattoir or knacker's van usually terrifies them.

INDIVIDUALITY

Of course, horses vary. They vary enormously. While horses all neigh for much the same reasons, some neigh more than others and all their neighs are different. The roots of their programmes, passions and fears are much the same, yet the relative strength of these feelings varies from horse to horse, and from time to time, and the way that they cope with them varies too. These character differences as shown at any point in a horse's life are influenced by:

genetic (hereditary) make up;

effects of past experience;

effects of present circumstances.

Hereditary variation It is difficult to estimate how important is the genetic contribution to character. From birth a foal is heavily influenced by his mother's attitude, but isolating foals from birth would not make their 'natural' character emerge more strongly since it causes so much disruption to the development of identity and social behaviour that it tends to produce abnormal animals. We have to rely on circumstantial round-about evidence, and most of it has not been analysed. Horse-breeders know that one family line tends to produce certain characteristics of temperament; Russian breeders state that the sire's character has more influence than the dam's; US studies show that aggressiveness to other horses follows the mother's character. It would be interesting t   ther fostered foals take after their mothers or their   ster-mothers, for this would show whether this type of aggressiveness is n.   d or learned.

'Character type' has been the subject of a good deal of work in Russia, following Pavlov's discovery that animals of different character types become neurotic more or less easily; this is discussed in greater detail on page 193.

The types of factor that are probably inherited are: activity drive (strong hormonal influence); tendency to flight; nervousness/boldness and excitability.

The broad character differences between breeds must be genetic. Thus Arabs tend to be nervous, active and excitable; cobs to be bolder, lethargic and placid, and thoroughbreds to be bold, active and excitable. There are, of course, bold Arabs and hysterical cobs, but the opposite is more usually true. Yet these generalizations about character types are again irritatingly vague and subjective since we are not sure how many independent factors are at work, nor how to make any attempt at measuring them.

To what extent these character differences are linked to physical differences is a difficult question. Nervous horses tend to be thinner than placid ones, echoing the endomorph-ectomorph range found in humans. But unhappy horses of whatever character type tend to lose weight too. *Eye position*, as well as differences in visual acuity, clearly influences a horse's information about, and attitude to, the world. *Coat colour* is an old saw: it is often stated that grey horses are more nervous, particularly at night; that chestnuts tend to be irritable; that blacks turn vicious more easily. It is true that chestnuts tend to have sensitive skins (they are far more prone to skin disorders) but to what extent the character differences are attributable to coat colour, and how much to the preconceived prejudices of their trainers, cannot be distinguished: horses are so sensitive to the attitudes of their handlers that they are quite capable of providing good evidence for all sorts of subjective notions, true or imagined.

Past experience interacts with genetic make up to give the horse a kind of working plan for behaviour. Since the genetic background varies, the effects of experience on character differ: thus severe handling will make a placid horse obedient, a nervous one terrified and an excitable, bold horse vicious; an experience that is traumatic and nerve-shattering to one horse will be shrugged off by another. As the effects of these experiences build they shape the horse's attitude and also his future experiences.

It is a mistake, however, to think that all a horse's fears and upsets arise as a result of unpleasant experiences. A horse's innate sense of self-protection leads him to be headshy naturally, and a trained horse that is still headshy or protective about his ears has not necessarily been beaten about the head: it may well be that his protective feelings are particularly strong and that the extra care and patience necessary to habituate him to being handled have not been applied.

Stereotypes, private games, likes and dislikes, idiosyncrasies and habits particular to individual horses make up a good deal of what is commonly called 'character', although they are not as fundamental to the horse's nature as the differences in spirit shown even in early training or in the wild.

Present circumstances Horses reveal different aspects of their characters according to how well their present conditions fulfil their needs, and what suits one horse, or even most horses, does not necessarily suit another. Happy horses are merry and alert, even if they are naturally nervous; unhappy horses are unhappy in different ways and for different reasons, according to their underlying character type.

Visiting a number of breeding and training establishments one is struck by the fact that in one place most of the horses are interested, in another bored, in another irritable, despite their coming from closely-related genetic stock. Similarly Soutar, a pig-keeping analyst, maintains that a stockman's character is evident from the behaviour of his pigs, while Patterson, a large-scale Hertfordshire dairy farmer, finds it more meaningful to rate his stockman's milk yield rather than that of his cows. When we look at a trained horse, whose character are we looking at?

8

Horses and People

Horses for a quarrel,
Camels for the desert,
Oxen for poverty.

(Saharan proverb)

For over five thousand years people have been involved with horses, through different civilizations and societies, and as their attitudes and treatment of each other have varied so have their attitudes towards horses. For the early nomads who first tamed them, horses were useful beasts of burden and drawers of loads, and as their size increased through breeding they became riding animals too. But above their mere usefulness horses have always appealed to the spiritual side of our nature, and in many societies their beauty, grace, courage and vigour came to symbolize a nobility that was worshipped, and even sacrificed, as godlike. Creating a harmony between two such divergent species, united in purpose and motion to their mutual benefit and delight, has fascinated horsemen ever since.

The horse's responsiveness to handling has ever provided a mirror to reflect our ideas, ambitions and philosophy, while his emotional life, as vivid and powerful as our own despite his lack of reasoning power, has similarly reflected our personalities and character. The wild Scythian horsemen of the ancient East gloried in the swooping swiftness of mounted raiding, while early agriculturalists harnessed the horse's sheer muscle power to help them till, harvest and trade. The writer of the Book of Job saw the horse as a reflection of God's power and glory; the Koran submits that 'every grain of barley given to a horse is entered in Allah's book of good deeds'. The Chinese Taoists, who understood and felt the flow and unity of natural processes and the straying of mankind from the Way, used the treatment of the horse to exemplify their philosophy of harmony; by running counter to the 'real nature of horses' Poh Loh in his arrogance corrupts and destroys them (*see page* 7). Sympathy succeeds where force does not: 'That which of all things is most yielding can overwhelm that which of all things is most hard,' says Lao Tzu, and he describes what might easily be two riders thus: 'The man of highest power does not reveal himself as a possessor of power; therefore he keeps his power. The man of inferior power cannot rid himself of the appearance of power; therefore he is in truth without power.'

For others the horse, like people, was an object to be broken, curbed and conquered: the peaceful species became the greatest instrument in the development of war. Yet even Xenophon, the astoundingly successful Greek general, embodied the ideals of his civilization when he wrote of horse-breaking in 400 BC: 'Anything forced and misunderstood can never be beautiful,' quoting the earlier Simon of Athens: 'If a dancer were forced to dance by whip and spikes he would be no more beautiful than a horse trained under similar circumstances.' Sadly this classical equestrianism which gave grace priority over success by force was lost, like so many other enlightened attitudes, in the Dark Ages, until its revival in eighteenth-century France. As the endless struggles of power-seekers tore Europe and destroyed civilians' lives, 'show the horse who's master' became the key to destruction of many a horse too. Yet there were always some, working men who took pride in their work and their horses, equestrian artists spellbound by the fascination of achieving harmony, or merely private horse owners, who maintained the ennobling tradition of sheer delight in a good horse enjoying himself.

In the twentieth-century Western world there is little work or war for horses, but our uses of them still reflect our greeds, needs and pleasures: as a source of income from breeding, training, dealing and so on, to win prizes for money, self-gratification or as recognition for some ideal of perfection, for the compelling interest of communicating with an alien life, or as companions and friends. As our aims and ideals vary, so do training methods, and a confusing plethora of dogma abounds. The common thread running through all fields of horsemanship, though, is the ideal of harmony, and while there are recognized and well-documented ways of achieving the balance, equilibrium, suppleness and health that are essential for physical coordination between horse and rider, the problem of psychic harmony remains.

The practically lost art of listening is the nearest of all arts to Eternity.

(Yeats)

Whatever we do with a horse involves a two-way relationship, not a one-way directive. The expert dressage rider, demanding the horse's complete attention, is not merely an expert commander but an expert listener too, being as aware of the horse's signals as the horse is of his. Channelling the horse's physical and psychological energies into the direction we want demands recognition of what those forces are, and respect for them too.

How, then, does a horse look at the question of 'breaking' and training?

HOW A HORSE LOOKS AT TRAINING

But the worst of all is that when his harness is once on, he may neither jump for joy nor lie down for weariness. So you see this breaking in is a great business.

(Anna Sewell, *Black Beauty*)

It is unfortunate that almost all the things we want to do with a horse run against his natural survival ideas.

Horse's survival programmes say:	*Our programmes say:*
no aliens on the back (*see page 48*)	ride
no aliens in the blind zone	walk behind or drive
run away when startled	not allowed
keep the feet free	grasp, clean, shoe them
do not get trapped	confine
keep the head free	tie up, restrain
stay with others	discourage
interact with others	discourage
use excess energy in play	discourage
explore, inspect	often discourage
groom self and friends	discourage when handled

When we achieve these aims we want to do even more unnatural and senseless things: hurl ourselves blindly over easily-avoided and absurd obstacles, endangering the feet; go round and round in circles, never arriving; or chase elusive balls round fields. Yet even wild horses become completely tame, domesticated, and not only willing to put up with our idiocy but positively interested in our schemes when we use the principles that are on our side:

1. *Habituation*, by which we accustom the horse to what we want in gradual stages, remembering that many repeated exposures to a stimulus are more effective than one long one. Here the maxim of Guthrie and the contiguity theorists is helpful too: *in any given situation the animal tends to do what it did last time.* Thus if we can engineer a situation where the horse wants to do something, we can precede his action with a cue and praise him for 'responding' so willingly. After several repetitions of this conditioning the horse still performs willingly even when he did not necessarily want to do it himself. This is certainly the principle on which to establish good feeling.

2. *Stimulus generalization*, through which the horse accepts our leadership and companionship as he would that of another horse.

3. *Sensitivity and dislike of imbalance*, which we 'shape' and refine into precise reactions to our aids.

4. *Reinforcement*, through which we encourage behaviour we want, and discourage behaviour we dislike.

S-T-A-T-E-S

There are six concepts that are of great help to the handler, rider or trainer, whatever his ultimate aim:

Signs from the horse;

Timing of actions and learning schedules;

Attention focus of the horse;

Tension in horse and handler;

Energy in the horse;

Space-value: position of handler in the horse's space system.

Reading the signs

Difficulties in communication with horses are often put down to the horse's inability or unwillingness to understand what we are trying to ask or tell him. But equally often the opposite is true: it is we who, absorbed in our views, are blind to what the horse is telling us.

In Germany in the 1920s there was a horse called Clever Hans who became famous for his apparent ability to read numbers, make calculations, and spell by pawing a certain number of times with his forefoot. His trainer, van Osten, was thought to be making some secret sign to tell Hans when to stop. But he denied it and, true enough, Clever Hans could still get most of the answers right even when van Osten was not there. But he did need an audience, as scientists investigating the case soon discovered, and the people present had to know the correct answers. How, then, did Hans read their minds?

Telepathy was not the cause: what Clever Hans was doing was watching for the slightest change in body-tension in the observers who, knowing the correct answer, unwittingly showed more interest in the number after the right one. Although this has been taken to show that horses are too stupid to learn to count, what remains impressive is just how clever Clever Hans was. How many of us could reliably use such tiny, unconscious cues from strangers to get the answers right? And how many of us could have worked out how to do it? Hans did so all by himself.

Clever Hans' sensitivity was astonishing – or rather, the kinds of signals that horses are used to interpreting are, to us, extremely delicate. The sensitivity of a highly-trained and willing horse is so great that we need years of training ourselves to be able to cope with it. And all the time he is feeding us information, showing us how he feels and what worries him, in signals that are often far too subtle for our word-oriented, self-absorbed, insensitive selves to notice.

Watch horses in a field. One walks towards another, stops, walks away again. Why? What was going on? Could you tell why the horse approached, what he was thinking of or why he changed his mind? Certainly both horses could because they read each other's signs. Was the first horse going up to the second one, or was he going towards something else and found the second horse in his way? Did he want to play, or to eat what the second one was eating, or to engage in mutual grooming, or to resolve a minor quibble? The possibilities behind even the simplest actions are almost endless.

As the chapter on communication showed, the different combinations of signals that a horse can be sending out are almost endless too. There is no simple way of defining every mood a horse can be displaying. A horse wanting to play approaches another horse – or person – with ears pricked attentively, a 'wanting-to' long nose, a jaunty, prancing step and high tail indicating high energy and excitement. A horse wanting to groom may well have almost the same face but will have the slouchy gait and lower tail position characteristic of loafing activities. A horse that is in mild pain looks quite similar to a horse that is irritated at the sight of you, but his ears and eyes signal attention in a different place – towards the pain source.

Plate 35 *What have we got here? This horse has been halfway round the Grand National course at Aintree and might be expected to be walking out with his neck outstretched: his nostrils and the veins on his face show that he still feels the exertion of it. But the oddness of giving a fallen jockey a lift back has perked him up. He throws back his head and minces along, raises his hip against the unexpected weight on his loins; his tail is kinked; despite the interest ahead he cannot commit his ears to a full forwards position. But his relaxed mouth shows that he is not afraid, merely amused by the queerness of it all.* (Photo: Louise Serpa)

Watching, absorbing, listening, is a major part of the horseman's craft, for it is only when we can appreciate what we are dealing with that we can achieve cooperation. Moreover, when a horse does not achieve that minimum cooperation from us she becomes afraid, mistrustful and resentful: we need to show that, even if we do not comply with her wishes, we do at least understand her signals of fear, doubt and need by directing our attention, however briefly, to their sources.

Timing

There are three sorts of timing that are important in dealing with horses: time of life; mood time; and micro-time. Failure to appreciate them is one of the commonest causes of failure in handling.

Time of life At different stages of a horse's life his natural behaviour patterns are developed to different degrees, partly because of experience but also because of maturation processes. A tiny foal, for instance, is enormously inquisitive and shows little of the fear of strange things that is so characteristic of an older animal: what better time to introduce ourselves as something that will be part of his life? A newly-weaned youngster, taken from his mother earlier than he would choose, still has a strong and unsatisfied following reaction. What better time to reintroduce ourselves as suitable objects to follow? Two- and three-year-olds are at the peak of their exploratory phase. What better time to allow them to explore and come to terms with the rich experiences of the outside world?

Working with the development of the horse's natural interests by asking him the right kinds of tasks at times when his tendency to do them is at its highest, tailoring the training to the horse's psyche, produces happily fulfilled animals whose willing attitude carries them through the more arduous training that may be required in later years (*see page 175*).

Mood time There are times of day, and weather conditions, and times in a young mare's cycle, which affect mood quite dramatically. To ignore these in a young horse is to court resistance. While pushing a horse for a little more than he wants to give may be good discipline, grinding him into a state of dejection or resentment because at that moment he does not have it to give is to turn him against us. Children will not learn under these conditions and nor will horses although, like children, they can sometimes be coaxed into a more willing frame of mind.

Mis-timing physical demands, when a horse is too unbalanced, too stiff or otherwise unable to meet them, also leads to mental resistance and resentment.

Micro-time Split seconds add up to years of work. Applying an aid at exactly the right moment, calling out 'trot' to a youngster a fraction of a second before he breaks, moving forward at the right time, are all critical. Watching a skilful trainer with a young horse one is barely aware of how perfectly timed each movement, each word, may be: the process looks effortless and easy. But watching the same young horse in the hands of an unskilled person may be an equally valuable experience, for then the mistakes in timing are seen more clearly.

Failure to read the signs of a horse's intention to do something is one of the chief causes of bad micro-timing, but it is also true that some people are not able to decide or to move quickly enough to be effective at the right psychological moment. As with the concept of space, merely being aware of the importance of timing is enough to make some mistakes obvious. *Conditioning an action to a cue does not take place unless the cue precedes the action by a mere fraction of a second.*

Micro-timing is particularly important in preventing unwanted actions. All learning theorists agree that punishment in itself is singularly useless in making an animal learn. It provokes pain and fear, which simply stop learning from happening. But it can be very effective in preventing an action if it arrives soon enough to prevent the action from being completed. Punishing a horse after he has bucked you off or run out from a jump is worse than useless: not only does it fail to stop the action next time, but it also upsets the horse since, having completed the action, he is now thinking of something else and has no idea what has provoked such sudden savagery. But hitting a horse on the rump just as he pulls back into himself to start to rear is effective, for it makes him leap forward and prevents the rear from being completed. When a horse is halfway through an action that we cannot prevent him from completing – kicking, biting – often the only thing we can do is to shout angrily. This is as unpleasant for the horse as it is for everyone else, and he is usually interested to find out whether it happened by mere chance or was connected to his action, so that he tries again fairly soon. Watching for the signs of his intention to repeat his behaviour, we can then be ready to apply punishment or ask him to do something else at the perfect moment, just before, or as, he begins to do it.

Attention focus

Since a horse has two eyes and two ears, his attention can be split in four different directions. The more important the subject, the more eyes and ears he will point at it – that is, unless his ears are signalling threat. Split attention can indicate confusion: when a horse stops with his eyes, ears and legs all pointing in different directions he is certainly confused. But the split attention shown by many ridden horses, with one ear on the path

Plate 36 *Split attention: Shakertown attending to the photographer and a mare at the same time.*

ahead and the other twitching back to the rider, merely shows a happy alertness to all that is going on.

In training, of course, we expect the horse's attention to be on us. The horse cannot respond unless she is noticing our signals. But when, for instance, a young horse is being lunged in an unfamiliar place her attention is sure to be everywhere else until she has had a good look around. Whether you call her attention to you, or simply wait for her to come back to you, will depend on the stage of training, the individual horse, and the excitement value of the surroundings. But one thing is certain: it is no use trying to tell her anything unless she is showing signs of listening to you first. Asking for a response and failing to get it is a short cut to having an argumentative horse.

Learning where a horse is looking unfortunately takes a little practice but often, very often, a horse that is 'refusing' to do something is looking at some particular aspect of it, or even something completely different, that frightens him. Thus a horse that unexpectedly refuses to get into a trailer may not be looking at the trailer at all but at, say, a coat flung over the door, a rope dropped on the ground, a flag fluttering in the distance.

If we ignore the 'danger' completely the horse usually grows even more baulky; but if we behave as other horses would and follow the line of his attention, we can indicate that there is nothing to fear and so reassure him. A horse feels doubly afraid when in the hands of somebody who refuses to listen to his warnings, and will often nudge the handler excitedly to try to force him to pay attention to the source of fear.

Tension

> The horse detests tension, for he must feel free and confident in his movement. The control of tension is the dominating factor in any sport.
>
> (Seamus Hayes)

Fear induces tension, and tension reduces sensitivity. Being able to eliminate tension in ourselves, particularly at the worst moments, is one of the first steps towards good horsemanship, for tension is infectious. Whether or not horses can smell fear we shall, alas, probably never know, but they can certainly see and feel tension in other horses and in people, and it scares them. If the leader is afraid, should not the follower be?

It never seems to occur to horses that they might themselves be the cause of our tension: instead, they look anxiously for the hidden tigers that we can presumably see. It is unfortunate for some people that, while not afraid of their horses, they have other problems and anxieties in their lives that they cannot help but reveal in their movements. Cultivating a relaxed bearing, an easy, unworried manner, is the key to winning the confidence of the horse, who is only too quick to respond to anxiety and upset. As everyone must know, tension makes us unable to control our movements delicately, unable to perceive things in their proper proportion, and unable to react sensibly. It does the same to horses.

While the signs of real fear in the horse, the rolling eyes, flared nostrils and panicky movements, are obvious to anyone, the signs of tension that reveal lower-level fear are less obvious. The first indicators of tension are the *mouth and neck*. A tense horse is stiff in the mouth, unable to move his mouth and jaw, and rigid in the neck too. In a ridden horse this produces a wooden feeling on the end of the reins. As tension increases, movements become stiffer, fluidity goes. A horse that is stiff and unmoving may be literally rigid with fear. (Donkeys, like rabbits, freeze with fear more readily than horses: often this is called 'obstinacy'.) At the lower levels of tension, he often cannot move his neck enough to turn and look at things, but has to roll his eyes instead. A horse that does not swing his neck freely

to look at the world about him is either half-asleep, completely trustful of his handler, or tense. Overdiscipline, the refusal to allow the horse to take his own interest in the world, produces tension, not attention: the confidence and trust that fix a horse's attention on us without tension are not arrived at through bullying.

A *stiff tail, bunched hindquarters*, and *mean, tight gaits* are also indicators of tension.

Signs of tension in a horse, especially a youngster, are interpreted by the wise handler as danger signals. The stiff mouth, stiff neck, stiff movements belie a state of mind where the horse may erupt into panic at the drop of a hat and damage not only himself but anybody alse around. It is unfortunate that many professional breakers, understandably anxious to produce a 'well-trained' horse in minimum time, produce instead horses that are afraid of doing the wrong thing and so are tense. Where breaking gear has been used neck flexion may be assured, but the lack of mouth movements which a relaxed young horse naturally shows as he salivates on his bit still

Plate 37 *Tension evident in neck, nose and mouth of this talented young Tennessee Walker (Pride's Immortal Maid) as she strains to perform to her best. The 'keg' shoes and rattling chains ('action devices') help to throw the weight of the horse backwards, thus releasing the shoulder, and stimulate high action.*

Less talented Walkers are less lucky. US Horse Protectection Regulations specifically prohibit various 'action' techniques being used in the show ring, though of course there is no control over what goes on in training. Among these prohibited techniques are: 'Injecting (any) tack, nail, screw, or chemical agent' (usually blister, now helped by DMSO and kerosene); 'burning, cutting, or lacerating' any limb of the horse; chains, etc. 'not free of protrusions, projections, corrosion or rough or sharp edges'; boots with sharp edges; metal hoof bands that can be screwed tight round the coronet, or that have projections that stick into it. And so the regulations continue, specifying brutality far beyond what one could possibly believe that anyone would do in order to make the horse lift its feet high and win prizes. Nevertheless, the regulations patiently list such devices (to the tune of 30 closely-packed sub-paragraphs) so their use must be common enough to warrant legislation. Showing scarred horses is also prohibited now, and so strenuous is the action that horses may not be worked for more than 10 minutes without a break, and 20 minutes in all.

The high tail carriage of Walkers, Saddlebreds and Hackneys is often obtained by: (a) keeping the horse permanently in a harness braced against a plate that forces the tail up and back; (b) docking the tail (now illegal in Britain) and fastening a false tail on the stump; (c) putting a lump of ginger in the horse's back passage just before he enters the ring. Stallions and geldings may also have their sheaths gingered to obtain flexion of the back legs.

Plate 38 *Justifiable terror in this petrified yearling being sold for meat is shown in his tight mouth, submissive ears and rigid neck. A horse that freezes with fear like this is liable to stand stock-still until fairly strong efforts are made to move him, when he will explode into violent, panicky movement.*

reveal the inner tension: adrenalin, the hormone of 'fear, flight and fight', dries the mouth.

Awareness of the signs of tension is a part of good timing, for it means that the horse is not rushed in his training but rather is allowed to relax at each stage before proceeding to the next. There is no hard and fast rule about how long each stage should take: where there is no tension, the horse is ready to move on. A surprising number of horses can be bitted, backed and ridden out within a day without being tense. A relaxed young horse, however untrained, naturally yields beautifully, though slowly, to delicate pressure on her tender mouth and sides: it is not a lack of training but tension in the mouth, neck and body that leads to resistance.

Causes of tension are high arousal in excitement, conflict and fear. A horse that stops to look at what might be another horse on the horizon quivers with tension, as does a courting stallion: both are half-afraid, half-desiring. These kinds of tension are not dangerous. But in a handled horse tension is usually due to sub-threshold fear. Watching the direction of attention focus tells us where the fear stems from; if it continues throughout training and under different circumstances then the handler should suspect that his own tension is causing it.

Energy

Wild horses, parasitized and underfed, maybe nursing one foal and carrying another, still choose to move from one place to another at a canter fairly often; in Montana some bands make a daily trip of twenty miles to water and back as a matter of course. How much more energy must a confined, unparasitized, well-fed horse have?

Many horses have a great deal more energy than is often suspected. Many riding school and trekking ponies habitually work six or eight hours a day on minimal feed, while the long-distance rides gaining popularity today are mostly not a great deal more than any honest horse would have done regularly a hundred years ago. An hour's work for a fit and healthy horse does little more than take the playful bounce out of him, yet until he has had a chance to work off his excess need to move about it claims so much of his attention that he cannot attend to much else.

Healthy children erupt out of school in a mindless burst of energy; young horses do the same. Giving the horse the freedom to use his surplus energy in play or in reasonably undirected free movement before attempting to settle to serious work allows some of the tensions that have built up in confinement to work themselves out. Far from creating problems of overexcitement, as is often feared, this policy sets up a pattern of free forward movement and strong impulsion that can be maintained as the demands on the horse's attention are increased. Too many young horses are not allowed to play or run about, which tends to make them either increasingly explosive or dull and resentful as their energy bottles up.

Some horses naturally have a good deal more energy than others. Arabs and stallions, both renowned for their stamina (or energy) are particularly prone to the explosive or hysterical behaviour typical of an over-energized animal. Punishing or attempting to quash excessive high spirits generally leads to no good; if the horse is too high to be pleasant under saddle then the need to run about and play can be allowed to work itself out on a long

strongly forwards
and upwards:
leap

static; but this horse
still shows 'forwardness' in his
attitude and stance

fast forwards:
gallop

backwards:
jib

free forwards:
desirable at all paces

strongly backwards
and upwards:
rear

lunge rein or by half an hour's free lunacy in the paddock or school. Sudden explosions of energy and playfulness must find an outlet somehow unless they are to turn against the trainer: trying to restrain the horse is less of a solution than asking him to use his energy until it dies to manageable proportions.

Weather also affects energy levels dramatically.

Space

A 'broken' horse is one which: accepts people within her personal space (individual distance); accepts a person on her back or a trap behind her; is relaxed enough to yield to pressure rather than fighting it.

Although it is possible to force a horse to tolerate a person's close presence by cornering her and handling her until her terror dies down, such a horse cannot be called truly broken, for whenever she has an opportunity she will put her individual distance between herself and her handler. Forced invasion of a horse's personal space is grounds for self-defence according to a horse's system, so that when she is loose she will move away and when she cannot do that she may turn her back and kick. Unless the horse has voluntarily accepted a person close beside her, she may resent the act of being approached and caught for the rest of her life, even though she may have learned that once caught she must behave in certain ways or punishment will result.

A horse that invites people within her personal space is a different matter, for once having accepted that closeness she treats us according to her social system: that is, she will mimic us, accept us as leaders, and tolerate almost anything else we care to do, though it may seem a little strange at first. In breaking wild or unhandled horses this principle is especially important.

A wild horse has two lines she is not willing for us to cross: the boundary of the flight area, and the boundary of the personal space. In a large pen or stable the horse has a limited freedom to run away, and can be allowed to

Figure 33 *Where the energy goes is just as important as how much of it there is. Thinking of the direction and strength of the horse's energy are especially important in riding when, for greatest efficiency and control, the horse should move freely forwards with his hocks underneath him. A horse that leans on the bit (often against an insensitive hand) becomes heavy in front, driving his energy into the ground; a horse that is 'above' or 'behind' the bit arches his back downwards instead of upwards and cannot get his hocks under him.*

Plate 39 *Cutting horse Doc's Oak shows superb appreciation of space and timing as she wheels and head thrusts at a cow trying to return to the herd. The rider, Tom Lyons, makes no attempt to direct the horse, which works the cow on her own, keeping her at this distance and blocking her return with swift turns and lunges. Although these horses are carefully taught to stop and turn quickly with their hocks right under them, training cannot give a horse the talent to cut cattle effectively: she has to have 'a lot of cow in her' or she has no interest. As one trainer put it: 'She's mad at that cow for invading her space.' 'Cow' seems to be a partially hereditary characteristic. Horses that turn out to have no talent are turned to other specialities (see page 176). (Photo: Louise Serpa)*

run until she accepts that a person standing quietly is no threat even if he is well within her ideal flight distance: once she is tired of running habituation sets in. Until the horse is relaxed enough to eat or scratch despite a person's presence within the flight distance she is not ready for closer contact.

Entering the horse's personal space can only be done on the horse's initiative, and unless she is bold, inquisitive or lonely enough to approach of her own accord (which is rare) then bribes are invaluable. While too much hand-feeding creates problems, here, for a little while at least, it is the only enticement strong enough to make the horse cross the immense barrier between herself and that little-known animal whose presence so far has always meant fear and possibly pain. If an isolated horse is kept hungry and not allowed food until she approaches, she quickly learns to come, and once we are within reach we can use the signs of friendship she knows well – mutual grooming, scratching and rubbing. Friendship established, she soon becomes unwilling to let us leave, and when we can handle her all over she can be halter-broken like any normal horse and safely released from her confinement.

A horse that genuinely accepts a person within the individual distance is virtually broken to ride except for the novelty and surprise attached to the idea. Days spent sitting on piles of cut grass waiting for the horse to come are not wasted: it may take even as long as a month before the horse is truly pleased to see and be near a person, and can have his hindfeet picked up and his tail scratched, but once this is done without tension he can usually be halter-broken, walked out and ridden within a few days in perfect safety. Horses that have been forcibly caught are seldom safe even after a few weeks of riding, for whenever they are startled they try to escape from the human presence once more. An accepting horse, however green, trusts his rider and tries to stay even closer in times of danger. 'Wild' horses are of course far less frightened of the outside world than domestic youngsters raised in confinement.

An older horse that refuses to be caught must also be enticed, by bribery if necessary, to approach: cornering him does nothing to remove his unwillingness even when he recognizes he cannot escape.

The concept of space is also valuable in free-schooling when by extending a hand or whip we extend our personal zone in certain directions to move the horse and turn him. A very friendly horse may lose all idea of space and refuse to move away; in that case we can take on some characteristic that recreates the boundary between us by making us temporarily unacceptable, like shaking a can, cracking a whip, making odd noises or even wearing strange hats. Striking the horse with a whip is better avoided if possible.

Space and free-schooling

In the United States, where Western horsemen traditionally broke horses the rough way in a 'bull-pen' – that is, a small, round, featureless corral, usually slightly larger than a big lunging circle, with solid high walls –

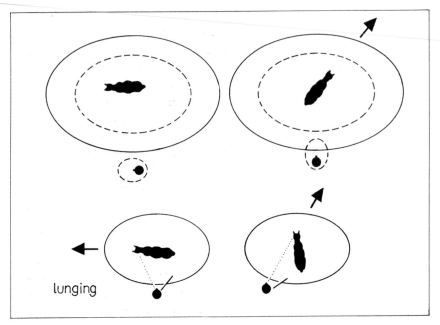

Figure 34 *People enter into the horse's space-system too.* Top: *The man on the left, walking past the wild horse without looking at her, goes by without entering her flight distance. But when he turns to face her, she feels threatened and moves away to keep her flight distance between the two of them.* Bottom: *In lunging the whip is used to extend our personal space so that it invades the horse's, threatening him mildly. The girl on the left is in the correct position: although the horse would like to move away at about the angle of the lunge line, she is holding him in so that he moves forwards. The girl on the right has got too far behind her horse and the lunge line is at an angle where it cannot control him properly: he is about to throw up his head and charge off in the direction that the whip is telling him to go, away from her. If she dropped the whip she would no longer be threatening him and would stand a better chance.*

several people have independently developed systems of early breaking and training that use the horse's understanding of space and signals to a high degree in free-schooling. Dr McCall, who teaches at Maryland University, uses body movements to control a young horse's movements: a stiff, tense, lunging action, like a horse's head-thrust and lunge, aimed at the horse's hindquarters, increases pace, for it is a threat-signal from behind; the same signal aimed in front of the horse mimics a body-check, causing it to halt, turn, or back up (*see Hamilton*). These simple, natural body signals are easily understood by a young horse if he has been brought up in a herd and not overhandled. To call the horse in, the trainer drops his aggressive stance and slumps submissively, even crouching if necessary. All sorts of refinement are possible through using the concepts of the space-bubble, threat and submissive movements, and infectious attitudes. Voice cues are enormously helpful too: hisses, combined with an upraised hand aimed at the horse's head, produce elevation without increase in pace.

These methods (there are variations) use the *horse's* signals and natural feelings to achieve a high degree of cooperation and responsiveness in a mutual harmony of movement. The importance of flexibility is easily appreciated here, for the 'handler' has no control at all except by feeling his way to the strength of body-movement that each individual horse will respond to; even a horse that has never been handled at all can be 'trained' to cooperate. Young horses seem to enjoy these games enormously, especially as the communication system becomes more refined and quicker reactions are asked for. The bull-pen, which constrains the horse to go in circles and centres his attention on the trainer – there is nothing else to attend to – is a valuable asset to those who understand the concept of space. The average British indoor school is unfortunately rather too large to use effectively: the free-schooling done for instance in dressage training has to depend on use of the voice and the whip rather than body signals, and at longer range the horse is less likely to respond except to a skilled person.

REWARDS, BRIBES, AVERSION AND PUNISHMENT

What a horse does under compulsion he does blindly. . . . The performances of horse or man so treated are displays of clumsy gestures rather than of grace and beauty. What we need is that the horse should of his own accord exhibit his finest airs and paces at set signals. . . . Such are the horses on which gods and heroes ride.

(Xenophon, c. 400 BC)

The threat of aversive stimuli is what keeps them alert. . . . A horse moves when slight heel pressure is applied because failure to do so in the past has been followed by a hard kick.

(Potter and Yeates, 1977)

From the manner in which rewards and punishments are administered, interesting conclusions can be drawn as to the character and mind of the rider.

(Podhajsky)

Rewards, bribes, aversion and punishment all change an animal's tendency to repeat whatever he has just done.

Rewards (positive reinforcement) come during, or straight after, an action and encourage the animal to do it again. The most immediate and obvious form of reward is food, though overuse of titbits as rewards leads to fussy, spoilt and overdemanding horses. However, once the horse likes to be handled he appreciates praise in the form of happy words and neck-scratching just as readily, especially if they have been connected with the earlier use of food rewards. A befriended horse works hard for praise, and his joy and delight in pleasing his trainer are wonderful to see. It is sad that many people do not realize how important praise can be to a horse: instead of encouraging the horse when he has done something desirable, they merely punish what is undesirable so that he is driven by fear. Such a horse may become as obedient as a robot, but he is not joyful nor, as Xenophon understood, beautiful. Moreover he may not be safe under circumstances that frighten him more than his rider's punishment does. The faith that occasionally leads horses to perform truly courageous acts only exists in ones that have been praised, as do the proud and willing attitudes that are such a pleasure to see.

How often do we see, for example, a horse or pony driven over jump after jump with no reward for her effort, though her mistakes are quickly punished? Most of us would soon go sour if we were treated like that. A word of praise as the horse touches down will encourage her better than a threat. We also see riders patting their horses as they receive a ribbon, which is useless: all the horse is being rewarded for is standing still.

In advanced training *relaxation* is a great reward. If a horse has once performed a difficult action, praise and relaxation are enough to make her repeat the performance next time. There is a danger in endlessly 'practising' a difficult manoeuvre, especially if it has been done for no reward, for after a while the horse grows to resent the pointless difficulty of it. Many resistances in training are created in this way.

Bribes are slightly different from rewards, for when they are used the horse can see the reward before he has done anything. They are valuable especially in early training for teaching the horse to approach, to come when called, to get into a trailer, to jump in a jumping lane, and so on. Really frightened horses cannot accept bribes, for their mouths are too tense and their minds are elsewhere; greedy horses will do almost anything for them; but some horses could not care less about them and remain steadfastly incorruptible.

Titbits Feeding of titbits, though well-meant, is unnecessary and often leads to trouble. Making friends with a horse is best done in the ways that are natural to him: by being relaxed in his company, by grooming him, and by speaking pleasantly to him.

Tone of voice is immensely important to a horse, and we can use it to praise, encourage, warn or punish. This cannot be overstressed.

Aversion or avoidance (negative reinforcement) teaches the animal to move away from possible unpleasantness, and is widely used in training. Many horses are trained only to avoid unpleasantness: they learn to move to a slight touch because they know and fear the spur, the whip, the pain in the mouth, the electric prod. To many people it is the only way of training, and they find it difficult to accept that there is any other: '[The transition from] escape conditioning to avoidance conditioning ... is the very foundation of horse training' (Fiske, *How Horses Learn*).

This is simply untrue. A large number of horses have not been trained in this way, and they are none the less sensitive and responsive. The more that positive reinforcement – praise and relaxation – is used, the less aversion is necessary; and conversely the less praise is used the more aversion is necessary or the horse never learns at all. But unpleasantness breeds fear, fear tension, tension inability to respond and thus resistance – and training becomes a desperate, dangerous and unpleasant struggle. While a young horse sometimes runs herself into trouble by, for instance, not responding to the bit but continuing to push against it until she becomes uncomfortable, the deliberate use of aversion as a teaching method is unnecessary and seems an expression of the worst traits of human nature. There is little that is desirable in a horse that is frightened into dull obedience.

> Positive reinforcement methods encourage positive attitudes;
> negative reinforcement methods breed negative attitudes.

Punishment (*see also page 42*) is often confused with aversion, and is often used at times when it will do no good. It can be useful for discouraging unpleasant behaviour that the horse has thought up for himself, like biting, but useless when trying to teach a horse a new action in response to a new cue: punishing a 'wrong' response frightens and confuses the horse and makes him even less likely to cooperate next time. (Getting a 'wrong' response to a new cue is usually due to bad timing: if the horse is relaxed and ready he will usually perform raggedly but correctly. If he does not then he is generally ill-prepared and punishment will not prepare him any better.) Bad use of punishment causes great resistances in training.

Harsh words are punishment to a horse that is used to praise, and the tension that invariably pervades our bodies when we speak harshly is also unpleasant to him. Hence the value of training by praise: even when our hands are full or we are falling off we can still say how much we disapprove, and the horse will mind and change his plan: a punishment-trained horse will be trying to escape.

More Xenophon: 'By encouraging him to adopt the very airs and graces which he naturally assumes when showing off to the best advantage, you have got what you are aiming at – a horse that delights in being ridden, a splendid and showy animal, the joy of all beholders .... The majesty of men themselves is best discovered in the graceful handling of such animals.' Those Greeks rode bareback into the horrors of war on hot little stallions: how many modern riders could do the same on aversion-trained horses? In over two thousand years, have we regressed?

Attitudes: submission, obedience or responsiveness?

When a horse 'does what he is told' we can look at it in different ways: we can say the horse *submits* to our will, that he is *obedient* to our commands, or that he *responds* to our signals. Each of these attitudes affects the way we go about riding or training.

The idea of *submission*, like the idea of a dominance hierarchy based on aggression, leads to difficulty. It is not the way that horses naturally think about relationships, as we have seen: they think in terms of friendship, kinship and signals. It is in competition that they submit, by moving away from each other's threats. Is moving away, then, to be the basis of our coming together? Is threat to be the framework of our harmonious relationship? For many trainers and horses it unfortunately is, which makes the horses understandably eager to escape the process altogether. Faced with any such 'rebellion' the domineering trainer sees no option but to treat the horse more harshly, to increase his threats. Even when the idea succeeds it produces a truly broken horse, a dull-spirited beast with no interest in the world or his work, only in avoiding unpleasantness. If submission is thought about at all, it must be in terms of attention, not aggressive threat.

Obedience seems a better tack, for the trainer then thinks of reward as well as punishment and aversion. The horse is taught simply that if he obeys all will be well, and if he disobeys it will not. The disadvantage here is that the horse is left no space. Unable to think for himself, he becomes confused or agitated when faced with new problems. The trainer feels no compunction to take notice of the horse's signals. This one-sided process, a stream of commands, is more suited to motorcycles than to living animals, and again it is not the way that horses naturally think.

Horses do think about responsiveness. They read each other's signals constantly, and they are very good at it. The trainer who thinks in terms of responsiveness is thrown back upon himself when the horse does not cooperate: he looks at the mistakes he may be making in his own signals, looks at the horse's signals too, and is more able to make the adjustments that are so necessary when dealing with such varied characters. He can pick up and develop the horse's ideas when he wants without seeing it as a breakdown in discipline. The horse, freed of the pressures of a bully or a sergeant-major, is interested in the problems facing her and is grateful for any suggestions that help her through them: she does not fight back, nor become an automaton, but uses her mind and indulges in one of her greatest talents, that of responding. The first two trainers would see such a horse as both 'submissive' and 'obedient'; but she is likely to become more sensitive, more intelligent, and more interested in life if we adopt her attitude rather than forcing her against the grain to adopt an alien one.

LEARNING SCHEDULES

In early training most 'learning' is *habituation* – getting used to being handled, to a saddle, bit and rider's weight. Habituation takes place most effectively if the response (in this case fear) is thoroughly removed in each session, and in repeated sessions (*see page 41*). Horses habituate more rapidly to a new stimulus when they first rehabituate to already familiar situations, so that a suitable set of sessions for a young horse will run through several known stages before a new one is introduced at the end of the session. This has the additional advantages of:

(a) using up excess energy in preliminary stages;
(b) rewarding the horse with relaxation at the end of each new step.

The aids Simple aids for turning and stopping, using leg, weight and hands are natural to a horse, for he is simply moving so as to relieve himself of pressure on various parts of his body or to rebalance himself. Moving forward to heel pressure is not so obvious, and here it is best to teach the horse to move to a voice cue earlier in training and use it together with heel pressure at first, or simply to wait until the horse is about to move forward and cue him if he does.

**A TENSE HORSE DOES NOT YIELD TO PRESSURE BUT
RESISTS IT.** 'Learning' the simple aids is usually just a process of
becoming less tense: a relaxed young horse responds perfectly adequately
even the first time he is ridden. If he has already been praised for moving
away from hand pressure on different parts of his body he will be well-
prepared for the idea. Overpetted horses often push back at first.

Exactly what form the aids take depends on the style of riding favoured:
the point of pressure determines which part of the horse's body moves.
The absolute rule here is that the aids should be consistent. Where a horse
has to be trained to do different tasks, and thus behave differently, he is
immensely helped by a complete change of Gestalt: a different place, a
different set of tack, a different bit.

The psychologist Moyra Williams successfully trained horses without
using a bridle at all, simply by applying hand pressure on the withers.

Later training may involve learning to respond to cues that are less natural
and obvious than the basic ones. Researchers at Texas University found
that in this type of true learning (they taught horses to back away from a
hand signal in order to avoid a shock) horses learned in fewer sessions
when trained weekly rather than daily: on average they learned perfectly
in 18 daily sessions but took only 7 when trained weekly. Remembering
the young horse's tendency to boredom, which leads to playful resistance,
we can safely reduce our training sessions for learning difficult movements
to a mere one or two a week and devote the rest of the time to enjoyment,
relaxation and suppleness, knowing that the horse will learn just as fast, if
not faster. Increasing the number of training techniques at our disposal and
using a little imagination so that training sessions are always varied also
overcomes the problem of boring repetition.

Learning to learn is an important idea. Young animals of all kinds have a
huge capacity for learning (their love of exploration might be seen as a
kind of greediness for new sensations) and the more they learn the better
they get at learning. In the wild, horses have plenty of opportunity and
become very quick-witted; but youngsters raised in domesticity in the
same unvarying conditions are often deprived of any opportunity to learn.
'You can't do anything with him until he's three' runs the popular mis-
conception. You might not be able to ride him, but you can involve him
in games and puzzles that keep his bright young mind alert and interested.
He does not necessarily have to be learning anything that will be of use to
him in later life: the fact he is learning at all is what is important.

Variety is the essence of it. Doing the same thing again and again is not learning. Who would expect a child to attack a problem intelligently if he spent years merely repeating his tables and not doing anything else? The young horse should be introduced to something new every time he is handled.

LIFE-TIMING AND TRAINING

As they grow up, horses change not only physically but psychologically, so that by timing our training suitably we can go with the horse's desires instead of having to fight them.

Age	Natural Processes	Suitable Training
to 1 month	unafraid of novelty follow mother	handling and halter-breaking following mother
6 months	following strong suspicious of novelty	halter-breaking and walking
1 year	independent exploration following play	walking out free-schooling games and puzzles
2 years	exploration strong submission to threat begins to wane	walking out, backing, long- reining, light driving, lunging more games
3 years	exploration independence movement from harem?	walking out riding out
4 years	settle down as adult	riding out begin school work
5 years	true adulthood little exploration	schooling

> There are nine-and-sixty ways of constructing tribal lays,
> And – every – single – one – of – them – is – right!
>
> (Kipling)

There are numerous ways of breaking a horse too (a horrible term, but its use is so traditional that any other seems odd), but some of them are more right, or more universally successful, than others. Usually there is heavy emphasis on work in the arena or school which can cause problems. It takes a good deal of skill and experience for a trainer to keep a young horse

Plate 40 *Beginning the way you mean to go on. This young foal (who looks more like a hinny than pure horse) is learning about ropes, traffic, shafts and carts at the same time as feeling quite secure beside his mother: the rope across his neck causes him no panic at all. As he grows up he will ease into his work quite naturally: 'breaking' and 'training' seem inappropriate terms here. Horses that learn in this natural way, however, seem a lot better trained than they are: trekking ponies that have learned to follow the tail in front and not to mind a rider's weight seem to be ideal children's ponies – until they are taken out of line, when their ignorance of any of the principles of riding becomes only too obvious. Mongolia.* (Photo: Louise Serpa)

interested in a school, and a bored young horse soon finds ways of amusing himself. A more 'natural' system is less likely to create problems, and can produce a horse that is just as 'well-schooled' to ride although he may never have seen a *manège*.

The young foal can be handled, taught to lead beside his mother, and have his feet picked up; his favourite rewards are neck-scratching and bottom scratching. Apart from a few days' socializing, he can well be left to the care of his mother: he will not forget these early lessons.

The weanling, isolated and afraid, is a perfect candidate for halter-breaking, for he will naturally follow a companion, even a human. His first walking-out sessions may be full of anxiety and hysterics; the presence of an older horse to follow is helpful at first. Once he is going well he can be led from a ridden horse or left free to scurry along behind: his following reaction will not let him stray far from a familiar voice and a larger horse.

The yearling will still follow, though he will do a good deal more investigating on his own if he is loose. These excursions are full of learning opportunities and satisfy the growing love of exploration: he can get used to bits of rubbish, traffic, crossing water, scrambling up banks and all the other difficulties that usually spook young horses. Walking out a large yearling can take strength; the youngster can be bitted and led on a halter rope slightly longer than the bit rope, which is used only in emergency. A yearling that has never been walked out will at first try to run away every time he is startled; later he will jump *towards* his handler as he transfers his social feelings and trust to him. A trustful young horse will lean one shoulder against you as he cranes round to peer at some strange new thing; while this, the natural bunching-up reaction of a startled group of horses extended to you as leader, is a very welcome sign, a demonstration of confidence in you, you may be knocked over unless you remind him of your desire for personal space.

From time to time a youngster will 'try' his handler, nipping or barging as he would his paddock companions. An older horse's reaction to this is fast and furious: so should ours be. Often he will be shocked into 'mouthing' respectfully. Feeble taps on the nose or rebukes that come too late are useless: a swift change from being a gentle companion to an outraged adult produces much better effects as long as the rebuke comes quick enough. Again, consistency is an absolute rule. A horse is never too young to learn manners: 'he doesn't really mean it', a cry often heard when a well-loved foal nips, is an invitation for a youngster to grow up obnoxious.

Familiarity breeds contempt: overhandling can make a youngster lose respect. Turning him out with others for months at a time teaches him good manners naturally, for older horses do not tolerate rudeness.

The two-year-old can also be walked out and accustomed to the variety of life. Over-protected children become nervous and timid: so do young horses if this time of life, their boldest and most exploratory, is not exploited. The youngster can be put through increasingly harassing trials more easily than an older horse, and as each one is surmounted successfully his confidence in himself and his leader's trustworthiness grows.

The two-year-old can be bitted, led or driven in saddle or harness, pull a harrow and taught to lunge; in none of these is he capable of real work but each novelty will be welcomed if he is accustomed to novelty. Games like carrying shopping bags, walking over sheets, eating in trailers and stepping over poles are excellent preparation for later life, for the horse is learning to learn. A strong youngster can be leaned on, backed, and even ridden for short spells on walking-out excursions in places he knows: he will come to like the experience especially if he is allowed to trot. He should not be ridden for more than a few minutes, nor sat on while he is standing still, for fear of damaging his back.

One of the most basic characteristics sought in a riding horse is that of *free forward movement*. Using the exploratory urge to its fullest builds a horse eager to see round the next corner, full of interest, impulsion and understanding, capable of handling himself. In an enclosed space young horses often feel inhibited, and have to be driven forward.

The three-year-old is traditionally the candidate for full breaking, as it is then that her back and legs will stand weight. Unfortunately it is also the time for her to be at her most independent. No matter how harmonious the training process has been, there often comes a moment when the three-year-old refuses to do something she is asked, with a 'why should I?' air about her. Understanding this moment, not mistaking fear for stubbornness, leads to fast and firm handling of it. Insisting is usually enough.

A young horse that has had enough experience of the world (and many have not) will not have the fear of novelty that is so common in green horses, and the breaking process will be free of the traditional traumas. Many horses change hands as three-year-olds, and the walking-out stage is still valuable here as a part of breaking, for there are few quicker ways of getting to know a new horse, what his reactions to novelty are, where his interests lie, and how he feels about people, than walking out with him. Watching for that moment when he turns to us in distress rather than trying to escape from our restraint, watching his faith and confidence build, we are far more likely to choose the right moment to climb on him for the first time than if we have merely worked him on a lunge until he is bored. Lunging is a deceptively simple technique, easy to do badly.

A horse that has been walked out can be ridden out almost immediately, and the more difficult the ground he is ridden over the more supple and well-balanced he will become. A young horse has not yet formed prejudices about where he 'should' be ridden, and takes more in his stride than many an older horse: he can be turned off a path more easily, sent up and down banks and through rivers, and take such a delight in it all that he goes forward freely and boldly. Open spaces are at first wildly exciting; in lanes and narrow paths a young horse feels too restrained to buck at a canter, while the path leads him ahead naturally. Hard ground and roads should be avoided, for the young horse throws splints easily. It is safer, where possible, not to shoe a young horse, and to ride him only as much as his feet can stand without soreness.

The value and techniques of schoolwork have been amply covered in many excellent texts; the value of the 'campaign' stage of riding – free forward movement over varied, even rough terrain – is often underrated because too many young horses have been overprotected and so are too frightened by it. But young horses easily become bored by arena work, and boredom means resistance and lack of impulsion. A great deal of 'school' work can be done in natural conditions with half the struggle that may be necessary in a school. The young horse can be worked round thistles and bushes to lighten him to the aids; he learns to balance himself better and get his hocks under him naturally if he is ridden slowly up and down slopes; rapid pace-changes or fast trotting round trees and bushes produce the same effect without nagging. A young horse that has learned to use his hocks in this way usually appreciates the feeling, and consistently moves better as a result. The trick is to find something other than ourselves that is making him make the effort: then we are a helping hand, not a demanding one, and the horse is educating himself naturally.

Further training There are so many different types of advanced training that at first they would seem to have little in common. All of them, however, require that the horse be of a suitable type, physically fit, full of impulsion, willing, and attentive to his job. Many types of training involve repetition of exercises, which is ill-suited to the exploratory nature of young horses. In higher training, then, we find the same general principles essential: variation in work to avoid sourness, perfect timing, and channelling the horse's natural desires to achieve a response rather than forcing the horse into it. The horse should be enjoying himself, look forward to his work, and take a lively interest in learning: any horse that is not positive about these things is potentially a source of difficulty, and the sensitive trainer will recognize the danger signals in his attitude before the horse starts acting badly too. Pressures on time and success may mean that the 'speciality' horse is only used for his speciality, to the detriment of his mental health. The active rider can find opportunities for training under almost any circumstances, and the greater the variety of circumstances he can use the sweeter the horse will remain, and the more reliable he will become. Thus, for example, the immensely valuable show stallions of the notable Arab stud illustrated on page 117 are used in cattle round-ups as well as in the show ring, and the benefits of their general education are shown in their calm intelligence in the hurly-burly of the show ground.

Horses for courses

You may not be able to make silk purses out of sows' ears, but they could be turned into serviceable pigskin wallets. There are many horses whose merits are underrated because they are not being asked to do the things they would best be fitted for. A timid (timid, not nervous) horse will not become a great showjumper, but she may well be invaluable as a pleasure horse for an uncoordinated rider, for she will tend to stop when she is uncomfortable.

By and large the hot-blooded breeds, thin-skinned and expressive, are thought to be more intelligent than the cold-blooded breeds. This is by no means certain: indeed, research at Texas University showed that young quarter horses scored better in learning tests than thoroughbreds, but it was only a single experiment and we cannot generalize too far from it. An intelligent horse may know perfectly well what to do but not feel like doing it, a common problem when repeating simple tasks is concerned. The calmer attitude of the cold-blooded type often makes her much quicker to learn, and quicker to grow bored and sluggish. A good bold cob can be bitted, saddled and ridden out within a single day, and show every evidence of having enjoyed the experience; the slow, reassuring methods necessary with nervous hot-blooded horses are inappropriate to a cob and tend to make him dull. Harshly treated, a cold-blooded horse tends to withdraw into stoic insensitivity where a hot-blooded one is more likely to grow panicky or vicious. Physical ability apart, the broad psychological differences between breeds means that they are appropriate for different tasks and different owners.

Intelligence is a quality that everyone would apparently want in a horse, but this is not so. 'You don't want too clever a horse [for jumping],' says Seamus Hayes, the renowned Irish showjumper of the 1950s and 60s. 'After all, a horse that knows the game is a fool to jump a clear round, for he will only have to jump again.' When they are doing things they do not particularly enjoy (which, as we have seen, is often) intelligent horses are much more evasive, and devious in their evasiveness, than stupider ones: many of them have no difficulty in outsmarting their riders. An intelligent horse is a wonderful companion, alert, inventive and constantly amusing, but he does not make a good competitive automaton.

Watching horses in a field together or at play reveals a good deal about their natural character (Is he alert, lazy, inquisitive, playful, bold or timid?) that working them may not, for the effects of training may mask their natural attitudes. It is only when we stop giving out instructions and start taking in impressions that we can understand and develop the horse's own natural talents.

Difficulties in training

> When his task is accomplished, his work done, throughout the country everyone says: 'It happened of its own accord.' (Of the wise leader's attitude. Lao Tzu)

Difficulties in training are the trainer's fault. 'Rogues' and 'intractable' horses occur far more frequently in the hands of bad trainers than those of good ones, whose success is often put down to their luck in working with talented material. Skill in training depends not only on good manipulation of the horse but also on recognizing undesirable tendencies before they actually become events: on sensitivity to the signs, awareness of the horse's character, flexibility and richness of technique and above all on willingness to accept responsibility for difficulties. It also depends on good riding.

Resistance is the major problem. Resistance to moving forward freely, resistance to stopping, to the bit, the leg, the right lead at a canter, being caught, to almost anything we want to do, recurs ceaselessly. In each case there are usually a number of reasons for the resistance, which makes finding the solution more difficult. A catalogue of possibilities might read:

1. Mistakes in

    space: standing in the wrong place, so that the effects of your body are not what you think they are.

    timing: asking for too much too early; moving too fast, too slow, at the wrong time.

    attention: horse is thinking about something else.

    tension: a tense horse *resists* instead of yielding.

    energy: an over-energized horse either plays or turns against his trainer.

2. The horse is

    bored (frequent, especially in young horses).

    afraid, because of lack of habituation to what is happening; unfamiliar circumstances; previous punishment; harsh handling; lack of confidence in trainer.

in physical difficulty: stiff, unsound, fat-necked, etc.
just plain stubborn. Often the first answer, seldom the right one.
3. Riding needs improvement
heavy or abrupt hands (often);
inconsistent aids;
inconsistent expectations.
4. Overbitting, causing fear of going forward.

Looking at the roots of the problem, rather than just the symptoms, leads to understanding, and the solution is then usually fairly obvious. Getting annoyed never helps, for it only increases tension in both horse and rider.

Boredom and *repetition* are potent sources of resistance: too much routine bores a young horse, who often decides to do something different just for a change.

Fear of strangeness is overcome by habituation. Again, too strict a routine often causes a horse to become afraid of experiences outside that routine.

Panics often occur at first. When a wild horse 'startles' at a danger, his companions do not rush up to him with soothing noises: they look to see what the matter is. A horse expects this, and directs our attention to the source of his fear. If we behave as a horse would and swing round to look, we can show by our calm and relaxed attitude that it is not a danger at all. Concentrating on controlling the horse is less effective, for if his warnings are ignored the horse usually repeats them in increasingly hysterical terms. Calm treatment of panics greatly increases the horse's confidence in our leadership: finding mildly alarming but not dangerous situations and handling them well is a good way of establishing trustworthiness as a leader. Competing for the Irish showjumping team in South Africa, Seamus Hayes was given a proven but unfamiliar horse, and astonished a crowd of watchers by never jumping him in practice sessions. Instead he rode him up and down a huge flight of steps, through the flags and buntings, and even into the refreshment tent. 'I knew the horse could jump,' he said, 'or they wouldn't have given him to me. But I wanted to be sure he trusted me enough to do everything I asked.' In the event, he won.

In the face of real danger, where an accident seems unavoidable, the best thing to do is often nothing: to stand relaxed, unmoving and unaffected. Creating a small nucleus of calm in the midst of panic can often save the situation entirely.

Physical difficulty If the horse is sound, fit and well ridden, physical difficulty arises from stiffness, lack of balance, tension, or bad conformation: if the horse can make the required action when loose in a field he should be able to do it when ridden. Riding up and down steep slopes and rugged ground is a great balancer and loosener for both horse and rider, and psychologically easier for the young horse than schoolwork.

Stubbornness can be a tricky business, for a young horse will occasionally disobey for no reason other than that he would rather be doing something else. Where force is used it may create tension which the horse remembers every time he comes to that place or movement. But there is usually no need for punishment: if we simply go on repeating the aids insistently without giving up *even for a second* the horse usually gives in quickly, and does not try it again. Habitually stubborn horses are ones which have been ridden by people who do not go on insisting.

Anticipation An intelligent, sensitive and willing horse sometimes starts to anticipate the rider's cues and act on them before they arrive. There are two main causes for this. Firstly, the same cues may have been repeated in the same place, or the same sequence, so that the horse thinks she knows what to do next. This is easily avoided with a little thought. Secondly, the horse may be doing a 'Clever Hans' and responding to the rider's involuntary preparations to give a signal, to the slight change of balance or tension that the rider gives as he thinks about the signal. (Many horses, for instance, rush off when a slack rein is shortened, since they know that this usually means that a 'go' signal will follow.) This type of anticipation is often welcomed in a pleasure horse as it gives that wonderful sensation of only having to think about something for it to be done, of telepathy almost. But in a dressage horse anticipation is most unwelcome, and here the only cure for it is for the rider to improve his riding so that he does not give out those preparatory cues.

Coping with resistance Once resistance has set in, for whatever reason, it is enhanced by tension every time the performance is repeated. Rather than repeating the same mistake – running into resistance and having to force a way out, thus making it worse – we can: (*a*) Drop the idea for a long while, concentrating on the roots of the problem though in different circumstances *or* (*b*) find different conditions where the horse must make the required movement though it is not us that is making him do it. Conditioning to a voice cue is also helpful. Where a horse is dangerously resistant (*a*) is the wiser course. Punishment is generally unhelpful.

For example, two common problems with young horses are resistance to taking the right (off) lead at the canter, and resistance to backing. With the first, we use (*a*): as soon as the problem shows itself, we drop the subject and concentrate on the root of it, which is that the horse is stiff on that side. (Most well-handled horses are, since they have always been invited to bend to the left when they are led.) Suppling exercises like lunging, or shoulder-in at the walk, cure the problem and when, after a couple of weeks, the subject is tackled again there will be no difficulty if the horse is truly supple.

With resistance to backing we would use (*b*): get a helper to push the horse back when the cue is given, using the word 'back' at the same time.

Resistance to the bit is caused by too harsh a bit and heavy hands. A young horse must feel free in front or she will not move forward. A thin metal bit hurts a delicate young mouth and makes the horse stiffen her neck and jaw tensely. Riding with a loose rein at first, and using either a rubber bit or one wrapped in towelling (well sewn on!), or strapping the bit into the noseband, make the horse more controllable, not less. A person who feels insecure riding a young horse on a loose rein should not be riding her.

DIFFICULTIES WITH A TRAINED HORSE

Fear, tension and resistance are the roots of these difficulties too, but in older horses bad habits are often so deeply engrained that the ways of eradicating them may be different.

When a new horse is found to have dangerous or frightening habits the first thing to do is to remember Gestalt. The horse's Gestalt, his whole world, changes when he changes hands, and often the root causes for the problem disappear too. Time is on our side: the more we relax in remembering that, the less tense we and the horse become. But even where the cause for a habit has disappeared it often takes an adult horse several months at least to drop the habits of a lifetime. In the meantime, encouraging and praising pleasant behaviour, and avoiding the circumstances that give rise to bad behaviour, reinforce the horse's positive attitudes.

A second general point is that horses with horrible habits are generally unhappy horses, mistreated, frustrated or frightened horses. Many have only been punished, never praised, and naturally dislike people. The more that this underlying misery can be alleviated the more likely the habit is to disappear, for the habit itself is merely the head of a boil: there is a great festering sore beneath it somewhere. Petting and titbits may be our way of showing sympathy but they are not a horse's: what a horse needs is activity, space and companions, and the nearer he can get to the natural state the less miserable he will be. He may have to be eased into it gradually, though.

Changing habits

Guthrie, the contiguity theorist, was particularly interested in the breaking of bad habits. Part of his learning theory was based on the fact that the more often an animal does something in certain circumstances, the more likely it is to do it again next time. Repetition, he found, was far more important than reward or punishment. Thus, preventing repetition is a major part of breaking habits. He gave three main methods of doing this:

1. *Using sub-threshold cues and rehabituation.* First, the circumstances are avoided altogether for a long time as far as possible, so that the habit is not repeated. Then one element at a time is reintroduced and worked with until habituation is complete: the idea is to split the situation up into small parts which singly are not enough to make the animal respond badly, and to make the animal feel comfortable with each one until the original circumstances can be recreated. This method works particularly well with fears and phobias: indeed, people with phobias are now successfully treated this way with behaviour therapy.

2. *Incompatible response.* Here the animal's attention is diverted with something more important so that other responses take over and are then repeated to form habits of their own. Bribing a greedy horse to put up with something he dislikes or fears replaces running away with eating, which he finds more important. It is in this way that punishment works: when timed right, it prevents the action being completed and breaks the habit.

3. *Fatigue.* This sounds contradictory, but it also works, especially with habits where the animal hoped to achieve some effect by his behaviour. The response is elicited again and again, and again until it is quite simply worn out. Thus a horse that kicks out of irritation when his rump or tail are touched can be made to kick fruitlessly for hours if necessary by a person standing safely beside him; a horse that habitually threatens people can often be stopped by simply ignoring the threats. The point is to let the animal learn that the action is fruitless and tiring. However, we do have to

be careful in using this method because it can verge on teasing, which might enrage the horse further.

The choice of which method to use depends on:

(a) the age of the horse (a young horse is likely to misbehave out of fear and lack of trust rather than calculation);
(b) how long the habit has been established;
(c) temperament of the horse (a high-spirited horse is more easily provoked than a calmer one);
(d) temperament of the rider (a method should not be chosen which does not accord with the rider's own temperament).

Byron Hendrix, a racehorse trainer in NE America, works with problem horses that have become so traumatized about the track that they cannot be raced. First they are removed from any signs of racing until they are calm to handle; then they are walked out and, when relaxed, shown a glimpse of his exercise track. Gradually he reintroduces the elements of the dreaded race: they are led along the track itself, exposed to tape recordings of the race, ridden slowly along the track, and so on. Habituation at each stage is complete before he moves on to the next. He has great success (and, like Seamus Hayes, he says that the more intelligent the horse the greater the problem).

Many problems can be cured in this simple way, and it is well worth the effort and patience required to set up a complete programme of stages to work through slowly. Habituation to each element must be complete before the next is tackled; tension is the sign that habituation is not complete. Rewards and praise for each success should be lavish, creating good feelings in place of the bad. Thus a traffic-shy horse may be fed from a stationary car; led round the car while the engine is running; driven by slowly on his own driveway, and then in a quiet lane, and so on. But at no point in the retraining should he be exposed to the full horror of the main road until he is completely ready for it. It takes time, planning, and often help from others too.

Evasion and napping Horses that have been ridden by timid riders are often evasive, and most can be pushed forward out of it by a confident rider. But a true napper, which whips round on a sixpence to bolt for home, is a different matter. It is a particularly sorry habit: what horse should not enjoy going out? Only one that has had a nasty time of it, surely. Increasing the nastiness by punishing the horse usually makes him quicker and more determined.

Here a combination of Guthrie's first and second methods can be applied: the horse can be taught that going out is not to be feared but can be fun. Anything aversive should be avoided at first, and any success rewarded. It is not difficult to find ways to make the horse want to go forwards: other horses, or even well-placed buckets, can be used to create new habits, and can be discarded gradually. This does not spoil the horse but retrains him, for when longer, solitary rides, or work, are reintroduced he will do them more willingly. Confidence in the rider, and pleasure instead of nastiness, are the keys to lasting success here. Forcing the horse may produce temporary success, but if the problem is deep-rooted then it will recur, sometimes in another, more dangerous, form. However, a change of hands, place, and work may be all that are required.

A ring-shy horse can also be treated with gradual habituation. To take a horse to a show merely to lead him in and out of the ring may seem a waste of time, but if it is pleasant for the horse it is the first rung on the ladder to success.

Bucking is usually due to high spirits and too much energy. It is a natural play move. Young horses also buck when unbalanced, or startled so that the rider becomes unbalanced. Horses buck from resentment, too, as when uncomfortable or whipped. Very few buck with the serious intent of removing the rider, and when they do they usually succeed.

It is not difficult to feel a buck coming, and it arrives in a sudden burst of energy that has to go somewhere. Channelling that energy, either by asking the horse to do something fast (turn, for instance) or kicking him on, prevents it from hitting the seat of your pants (incompatible response); trying to stop the horse altogether often makes the buck higher. But the best treatment for a habitual frisky bucker is removing the desire for it before the horse is ridden, by encouraging him to get it out of his system in playing on a lunge line or in an arena. If the horse will not buck, sacks can be tied to his saddle, and when he is tired of trying to buck them off he is ready to be ridden.

The very few horses that really buck savagely, with intent, have a complete aversion to being ridden and must be regarded as unbroken. The whole breaking process can be repeated, with an emphasis on confidence and lack of tension; a complete change of Gestalt and methods helps too. Again, every small success should be rewarded.

Rearing is fairly common in stallions, both ridden and unridden, for it is a natural part of their fighting or mating display. Often they rear because

Figure 35 *Rearing is part of a stallion's display (this stallion is theatening to fight an enemy stallion) and is thus a normal behaviour pattern, often seen in play in stallions. However, many stallions find it a successful and handy way to behave at other times too.*

they want to go forward but are not allowed to, so that they rear and leap at the same time. But in mares and geldings the vicious rear is the complete opposite of the free forward movement that is so desirable. Riding the horse with a good deal of impulsion reduces rearing, since a rear involves pulling backwards. Bitting is often the cause: a harsh bit makes a horse afraid of going forwards, so the bit should be as soft as possible. Strapping the bit into the noseband so that a hard pull works on the nose as well as the mouth often helps. Heavy hands breed rearers.

When a horse rears, fast action is essential or the rider may pull him over backwards (the rider's fault, not the horse's). Thrusting the hands as low as possible may prevent a rear developing, as does anything that drives the horse forwards fast. The old books advocate hitting the horse over the head with a bottle of water, but do not explain how to manage this in the heat of the moment. Nevertheless the same principle – making the horse think he has run himself into trouble as a direct result of his action – can be used in biting the horse as hard as possible on the crest of the neck while rearing. It has great surprise value. Often the horse tries again fairly soon to see whether it has the same results (*see also page 153*).

The sore festering beneath the rearing habit is lack of forward movement, which must be tackled if the problem is truly to be solved.

Jibbing, or refusing to go forward, easily develops into rearing if the causes for it are not found and removed. Fear and overbitting are the most common of these.

Biting is again mostly a stallion's trick and in them is usually due to sheer frustration from over confinement. In other horses it is a deliberate attack, though in young or spoilt horses it may be simply lack of good manners. A swift punch in the nose as the horse attacks is precisely the use of punishment that psychologists would approve, since it prevents the action being effective and leads to another – withdrawal. Allowing the horse to run himself into a sharp stick is also effective *but the horse must not be attacked with it* or a full-scale fight may develop: the principle is that if you were a hedgehog or a cactus the horse would soon learn not to bite.

Horses that bite when the girth is tightened can be fitted with a padded girth; they are often thin skinned, as are those that bite their riders' feet in irritation at the slight tickle of a trouserleg.

When a horse attacks people, the question to ask is: why? If biting is prevented in a vicious horse, he will think of some other form of attack unless the reasons for it are removed.

Kicking is a form of defensive attack, which means that the horse is defending himself against a presumed attack from you. His attitude towards people needs changing. Many vicious kickers have been so severely beaten for it that they appear to think that a person should be disabled before he has a chance to harm them. A really confirmed kicker should not be given the chance to kick while the readjustment of his attitude takes place; if by chance he corners you and is clearly about to kick, the best defence is to leap straight at his bunched hindquarters, for a kick at close range is far less disabling than one that catches you at full stretch of the horse's leg. Moreover the surprise move may actually stop the kick, but it does take great presence of mind.

Three major reasons for kicking are because:

the horse is still afraid of people in his blind space. More handling and habituation required.

the horse has been too severely punished and feels attacked: general change of attitude required. No more punishment.

the horse is irritable about having his tail or hindquarters touched: the *fatigue* method works well here, the horse being made to kick fruitlessly until he does not bother any more.

As with other bad habits, the cause must be analysed before a cure can be attempted.

Running away is one of the horse's strongest natural tendencies, and once the programme is activated it is difficult to replace it with a different one. Horses run away for different reasons:

1. *For fun.* This is an energy problem: the horse needs more work, or an energetic play session, before going out. Many horses simply want a good gallop when they first go out, and will settle quickly if this can be arranged; others become more excitable.

2. *Out of habit.* Because of previous training, as in ex-racehorses. Here retraining with slow work in enclosed spaces so that the behaviour cannot occur at all is indicated.

3. *True 'bolting'.* Horses are often accused of bolting when they are merely carting their riders off. True bolting occurs in a horse whose barely controlled fear suddenly erupts and sends him off on a one-horse stampede. When he is in this state anything that happens tends to make the horse go faster. This is a tension problem due to incomplete breaking, incomplete habituation. It was far commoner in the days of crudely broken driving horses, for a driven horse that starts to run is pursued by a hideously rattling trap.

4. *Bad riding.* Many people get carted off by energetic horses simply because they do not use the right ways of stopping. A determined horse cannot be stopped by a tense rider whose weight is forward; nor can he be stopped by a steady pull. Throwing the horse in jerks from one side to the other breaks the rhythm of the gallop and slows him better.

Riding or driving a horse that is known to run away is a frightening experience, not least because once running a horse can barely see and is liable to cannon into fences. But the more that fear and tension pervade the rider the worse the effect on the horse. A relaxed horse takes a second or two to get himself together, which is long enough to stop him; but a tense horse, with his neck and jaw resistant to the bit and his hindquarters under him, can shoot off at any moment. Thus riding the horse collected, on a short rein, is likely to be the worst thing to do.

If the horse cannot be stopped by other means, turning him in ever-decreasing circles slows him. Another deterrent is using the *fatigue* method: where the place is right and the horse fit enough, he can be forced to go on until long after he has had enough galloping and will think twice before trying again. This is not suitable with young horses.

Paranoia. People often feel attacked or threatened by their horses when there is no cause to be, and this creates problems between them: if the rider has no faith in the horse, how should the horse have faith in the rider? Where one is suspicious and fearful, should not the other be? Out of carelessness or lack of thought for us, horses often hurt or frighten us with no evil intent: unable to see with their heads tied up, they tread on us by mistake; they roll in sand or cool streams to relieve their itching, not to break our legs; young horses, aware of their size but not allowing for ours, scrape us against posts or under low branches; and they buck with delight on a crisp morning. In these ways they act innocently, thoughtlessly – at least at first. But a horse that is treated with suspicion is uneasy in human company because he is surrounded by an atmosphere of tension and fear, and such a horse will soon learn to use these moves deliberately in order to get rid of us and our unpleasantness. Thus, one of the quickest ways to make a horse evil-tempered and evil-mannered is to suspect him of evilness; and similarly one of the quickest ways to improve the feeling between us and the horse is to start ourselves, by thinking him a pleasant (though thoughtless, maybe) fellow.

People who work with 'problem' horses frequently find themselves at a loss to know what to do because in their confident, trusting hands the horses have no problems.

> There are no problem horses; there are only problem owners.
> (Hartley Edwards)

Riding. Many of us who have been riding for years are thoroughly experienced horsemen, but we may not be technically all that good as riders. It is a hard fact to accept: we tend to blame the horse first. The quickest way to find out who is causing the problems is to hand the horse to someone else whose riding we admire, and watch the result.

Overbitting. Heavy hands and insensitive 'contact' are common and cause a variety of problems: fear of going forward, jibbing, rearing, stargazing and panics. A horse will not move freely unless he is confident that his mouth will not be hurt. Reducing the severity of the bit, and using a lighter rein, decrease the horse's fear and resistance and thus increase control. A surprising number of horses, particularly timid and sensitive ones, can be ridden on a noseband, without a bit at all.

Travelling. Some horses have a deep and bitter hatred of travelling. While there are successful ways of forcing such a horse into a trailer, it is a dangerous thing to do if the horse loathes being in there. It would be better to ask if there is anything we can do to help him. Dr Sharon Creigier has made this a subject of special study.

Tellington, a Californian trainer, made careful measurements on the physiology of travelling horses and found that in a normal, forward-facing trailer they had greatly increased pulse rates, together with other signs of extreme fear like sweating and nervous dunging. Moreover they are under physical stress too, for every time the vehicle brakes they tend to tip forward. But when they face backwards (which they will always do if allowed) these signs of mental distress are not present, and when the vehicle brakes they can cushion themselves on their rumps. These results were also found by independent workers: Holmes, a New Zealander, designed a trailer on the strength of his results, and found it virtually accident-free. It is surely time we eliminated this appalling stress and allowed horses to travel the way they want: facing backwards, watching the landscape slipping away behind them, physically and mentally balanced. For the most part, we need better-designed trailers: a horse loaded backwards into a normal trailer must have his head protected by a head-bumper lest he throw it up at the vital moment.

A young horse should not have to make her first journey alone. Either another horse, or her handler, should be with her, though a person must be sure he can get out of the way if she panics.

Stable vices The classic 'stable vices' of wind-sucking, crib-biting, weaving and walking the box are distortions of natural behaviour patterns which have become ritualized into stereotyped habits. Crib-biting and wind-sucking derive from eating and swallowing; weaving and stall-walking from ordinary locomotion. Once they have become well-established, these vices are virtually impossible to stop except occasionally by mechanical means. This, of course, does nothing to remove the cause nor the horse's desire to do them. They occur in high-energy horses kept confined and fed on concentrated food, and may spread infectiously throughout a stable yard. All stable vices are debilitating because horses that suffer from them do not eat or rest properly. They do not develop in similar horses kept at pasture.

As these vices occur mostly in high-performance horses, particularly racehorses, their cost in purely economic terms is significant, and it is surprising that we know so little about them. Dominic Prince, who has begun pilot studies, found that among English racehorses as many as 20 to 35 per cent of the horses in one yard suffer from vices of one sort or another. He points out that in natural conditions horses crop with their

Figure 36 *The weaving horse stands with his front legs slightly splayed, shifting his weight from one side to the other in a rhythmic figure of eight movement that seems to mesmerize him. To watch, the action is as upsetting as the ceaseless rocking back and forth that some disturbed small children do when squatting on their heels: the animal seems to have withdrawn into itself in hopelessness.*

front teeth for many hours a day, and that their small stomachs are nearly always full of low-energy food. In crib-biting this same cropping action is made, while wind-sucking fills the stomach full of air. Both these patterns occur only in horses kept on concentrated food which does not allow the natural behaviour to be performed. Like bucket-fed calves which suck each other's ears, tails or mouths, they still have an unfinished programme that needs completing. His hypothesis explains why these peculiar patterns arise better than does the usual one, which is that they are caused by sheer boredom. While boredom may be a predisposing factor, it seems curious that horses should almost always choose one of these stereotypes to relieve it. Following his line of thought, we may be able to attribute weaving and stall-walking to lack of the right type of exercise; it may be that the frustrated need for company aggravates this restlessness.

> Attempting to solve the problem by physical means is rather like pulling out the fingernails of a person who chews them.   (Prince)

Like all good scientific ideas, this hypothesis gives us specific questions for future research: do horses that are kept just as confined and bored but given bulk feed develop them? Do horses that are exercised more slowly, for longer periods, develop these locomotory habits? To what extent is boredom a factor – do horses that are given footballs, plastic bottles on strings, or other toys develop them? Does company help? Is heredity a predisposing factor? In the absence of further research, we are left with a large number of obsessive, incurable horses and no certain means of preventing more of them developing these debilitating habits – except by keeping them in conditions more like those for which they are so well adapted.

Giving a horse space

Overdiscipline, as well as overconfinement, can lead to explosive, dangerous horses. Unfortunately when a horse starts to develop such tendencies he is usually treated with fiercer discipline, until in order to preserve his identity and his hide he starts to fight seriously. Stallions are particularly prone to this sequence, since many of them are overfed and underexercised.

To deprive a horse of every quality of his life that is natural to him is strain enough on his system; to expect a spirited, energetic horse to become totally submissive at all times as well may impose too great a strain. Where a modicum of discipline fails to work, increased use of the whip and curb probably will not either, and may pressure the horse into being sly, evasive, hyper-excitable or just plain angry. The problem is not lack of discipline or respect: it is that such horses are unable to get any relief from the demands of their bodies, because they cannot perform the programmes that would naturally give them relief. Mentally they are fish out of water, thrashing about uselessly. Their demands become so urgent that nothing short of pain will turn their minds from them. These horses need mental and physical space to make a few of their own choices, and no matter how rigorous their training, particular times and places can always be arranged for this. A horse that is treated in this way – that is, allowed to be a horse from time to time instead of a puppet – does not take advantage of this space: rather, he becomes more manageable, more relaxed, because he is free of those internal pressures. A sandpit to roll in, a companion, time out in a paddock, a bite of grass after work, and long, varied hacks, are small indulgences that mean a great deal to a confined, overdisciplined horse.

Not all horses become explosive in these conditions: some become dull and listless, others sour to their work, and some become stupidly nervous. The horse's character makes his misery take different forms, some of them more difficult to spot than others. But when we think of the horse in his

Plate 41 *Chinese gentleman (evidently not a disciple of Poh Loh) and his horse enjoying their own pleasures in their different ways. Such moments of relaxation and enjoyment are of great value to the horse's mental balance, dispelling the strains of an unnatural life. Horses, after all, do not mind if they are muddy.* (Photo: Courtesy of the British Museum)

natural environment, and of the way he behaves there, we can check to see where the arrangements we have made for him are lacking, and do something about them.

NEUROSIS AND NERVOUS BREAKDOWN

In an extensive study of personality difficulties, Dollard and Miller characterize the neurotic by three main features: he is miserable, because of his conflicts; he is stupid about some aspects of his life; and he has symptoms. The neurotic horse, too, is miserable, either hyper-tense or listless; he is stupid in some circumstances, behaving as if he is incapable of learning or throwing hysterics when there is no real cause; and he shows symptoms ranging from a constantly upset digestion to startling and sweating for no reason.

What makes a horse neurotic? One root cause of neurosis seems to be chronic, unavoidable conflict. That there is no way that the animal can deal with chronic conflict except by becoming deranged (which is not really dealing with it) is not surprising, since animals in the wild probably do not experience it: when conflict occurs they resolve it or walk away. Only in domestic conditions are they forced back into the same insoluble crisis again and again. In most cases the conflict is between fear and fear: fear that makes them want to run away and fear of running away because of the pain that they know would result. Another common type of conflict arises when the animal is given a signal that confuses him, so that he is afraid of doing the 'wrong' thing and being punished for it but also afraid of not doing anything because he would be punished for that too.

The fact that many horses do not display fear obviously but rather become tense, shrinking and withdrawn explains why owners and trainers can repeatedly allow the condition to arise: anyone insensitive to tension would not necessarily notice the stiff mouth and neck, the flattened tail, the slightly wooden movements, that are characteristic of it. The horse might, in fact, appear to be merely 'nice and quiet'; where handling has been over-harsh he would be anxious to be obedient, so that at first there might appear to be no problem.

The second major cause of nervous breakdown is trauma, as in a horse that has had an appalling fall or accident. In these unhappy creatures the fear that should rightly be associated with the incident overflows into other areas, pervading and corrupting other unrelated forms of behaviour.

It was Pavlov who first identified these causes of neurosis. He became interested in nervous breakdown after the Leningrad flood of 1924, which invaded the basement where he kept his experimental dogs in cages. The dogs were submerged for hours with only an inch or two of air at the tops of the cages to breathe. After this horrific experience several became totally neurotic: not only their reactions to water but also their behaviour in most other fields, such as learning, were deranged.

In an attempt to find out more about neurosis, which at the time was a rapidly-expanding field of research, Pavlov produced it experimentally through conflict: he conditioned dogs to respond positively to a circle but negatively to an oval. Then, little by little, he elongated the circle and rounded the oval until they were hopelessly confused. A different type of conflict was later used by Masserman, who trained hungry cats to open the lid of a box to get food when a buzzer sounded. When they had learned well, they got an air-puff in the face (which they hate) as they opened the box. In both cases breakdown – restlessness, extreme nervousness, inability to feed, and so on – resulted.

Pavlov found that it was much easier to make some dogs neurotic than others. Some resistant dogs simply ignored the confusion, remaining self-protectively aloof while others had turned into raging savages and yet others into whimpering dolts. He realized that personality type had a good deal to do with the result, and divided his dogs into four distinct types which, by coincidence more than deliberate design, agreed with the ancient Greek classification of character. The first two break down much more easily than the last two.

> *choleric:* aggressive, hasty bristly type of dog, which in experimental conditions becomes overreactive, savage and vicious to experimenter, passerby and chairleg alike.
> *melancholic:* gentle, timid, whiny type of dog which becomes withdrawn, overanxious and afraid of everything.
> *sanguine:* strong, well-balanced, agile, lively: this type continues to respond to the cues even where they are deliberately arranged to confuse it.
> *phlegmatic:* strong but inert, easy-tempered type, which stops reacting at all when attempts are made to confuse it.

We can recognize these types among horses too: the choleric types, bold and irritable, are easily turned vicious; the melancholics are those timid, unconfident, miserable ones that turn barn-sour and hopelessly nervous; the sanguine ones are the 'honest' horses that continue to try in all circumstances, while the phlegmatic type is most often seen in the duller type of cob (and in many riding schools).

Later work at the Pavlov Institute confirmed these generalizations. Popov (*see page 29*) quotes research by Andreyskas, in which horses had to learn rapid reversals of difficult choices. Four types of horse were recognized. The strong, balanced (sanguine) type, which adjusted quickly to the new choices, was also the best adjusted in the stable, at pasture, and in training. The inert (phlegmatic) type was characteristically non-reactive, both in the experiments and in normal life. But some horses, which were noticeably uneasy and overreactive both in the stable and when handled, found the reversals difficult and became hyper-excitable in the experiments: these were of the unbalanced choleric type. Finally there was one poor horse, noted as a weak, inhibited character, which broke down completely with total disruption of all her reflexes: a true melancholic.

Bobylev, who tried to put these findings to practical use, studied two responses in performance horses. First, he put the horse into a new stall, with food, and watched it; secondly, he sounded a loud siren when the horse was feeding normally in its own stall. His horses fell into three clear groups. Just over half of them investigated the new stall quietly and calmly, were soon satisfied, and quickly turned to eating. In the siren test they raised their heads briefly but soon started eating again; the next time it sounded they barely reacted. These horses were far the easiest to break and train. A second group, about a quarter of the total, did a great deal more investigating in the new stable. Although they were calm, they were careful to examine everything, for 5 minutes or more, before settling to feed. These horses also habituated fairly quickly to the siren, although their reaction to it was far stronger than that of the first group. By the third time it sounded they were barely pausing in their eating. The third group had much stronger nervous reactions. In the new stall they reacted violently, startling, trembling and snorting; only rarely did they eat, and they would not settle to it. The siren produced a strong response the first time, and stronger reactions each time it sounded; finally the horses refused to eat at all. Bobylev felt that a prolonged noise would produce nervous breakdown in these horses, all of which demanded far more time and skill from their trainer than the first two groups.

As in a good deal of Russian research, these investigators do not give exact details of their methods and results. However, these experiments (which surely deserve repetition here) do suggest that simple tests might characterize a horse rapidly. Ippolitova, another researcher, later used a test which simply involved tying the horse in a new stall and measuring its pulse rate. The common thread running through all these tests is how fast the horse habituates to strangeness and change. As we have seen, a good deal of training involves habituation; and trainers know that horses that are difficult at first are liable to give problems for the rest of their lives unless handled with extra sympathy and care (when they may turn out to 'give' more), while the easy ones generally go on being honest. But a well-trained horse of whatever character will perform reliably at home (when seen by a prospective buyer, for instance) and, if only seen when handled, give little clue as to his future potential in different and changing circumstances. Similarly a badly trained or handled horse will give a poor account of herself, no matter how adaptable her character. At the moment it is only years of experience, often hard won, that teach us the difference between the two.

Causes of breakdown

Kurtsin, who continued Pavlov's line of research with dogs, listed other conditions that produce neurosis and breakdown:

(a) long negative (unpleasant) stimulation;
(b) frequent negative stimulation;
(c) conflict: presenting positive and negative cues at the same time;
(d) confusing the animal about what it 'should' do in response to a cue;
(e) associating food with fear.

He also noted that in neurotic animals healing, as well as other automatic body functions like digestion and sweating, is affected: burns and other wounds take two or three times longer to heal than in normal animals, while ulcers are common.

The keys to neurosis and nervous breakdown, then, are: *conflict, confusion*, frequent *punishment* or *aversive* (unpleasant) cues, *trauma*, and *character type*. While most of this work was done on dogs and cats in carefully controlled laboratory conditions, the results apply in general to other mammals. These unpleasant experiments were not done for sadistic reasons but rather to gain an understanding of breakdown so that it could be prevented. The implications for us in dealing with horses are clear:

(a) cues should be clear and should always mean the same thing;
(b) we should avoid presenting two conflicting cues at the same time (this is quite often done by mistake);
(c) we should avoid training by punishment and aversion;
(d) we should make sure a nervous horse can eat in peace
  especially when dealing with highly-strung, spirited and excitable horses.

Treatment

Where a horse has become so neurotic that his bodily functions - digestion, skin health, healing, etc. - have become disturbed, the first step towards health is rest and removal from stress. 'Resting' in a confined space is not relaxing to a horse: he needs the things he has evolved for as a free-ranging social animal - space, companionship and interesting, even if physically tougher, surroundings. The 'melancholic's' companions must be chosen carefully so that the horse is not further harassed by aggressive, bossy types. After several months he may gradually be able to start being handled again, with an emphasis on gentleness and lack of pressure; as far as possible the conditions and surroundings that made him neurotic in the first place should be avoided. Some horses do not ever recover fully: that is, they are all right if left in natural conditions, but break down again at first signs of work. Others recover enough to be retrained to types of work they have not done before. Even where the process runs smoothly, rehabilitating the neurotic takes at least a year and often several.

Case histories

The *case histories* of some difficult horses show the causes and symptoms of behaviour problems, and the ways in which they can be helped. 'Treatment' usually meant arranging their lives so that their bewildered minds had some satisfaction and comfort before any demands were made upon them. All the time the horse's terrors and hatreds were kept in mind, so that battles could be avoided by avoiding those areas, and the habits of a harmonious relationship could be built up. I have chosen horses I knew well personally, but many horse owners will know similar cases (*see*, for example, Margaret Cabell Self). For the general reader these cases are interesting because they had to be helped in extremely difficult circumstances: we had no school, no flat training ground, no special equipment, and only steep and dangerous mountainsides to ride on.

Mangas Colorado was a handsome 14.1 black and white cob with an extremely intelligent head and eye. When bought, he was destined for meat; he was appallingly overweight and had had numerous bouts of laminitis through being left in lush pasture for four years. His previous history was unknown. He was highly schooled but explosive, given to running away, leaping forwards uncontrollably, and rearing mildly. He was impossible to catch and hated his mouth being touched at all. Putting his bridle on was a desperate struggle. He kept his tongue firmly over the bit and any effort to prevent him made him sweat and leap about violently. His nose and mouth bore scars from a drop noseband or grackle. He was peculiar about his food, sometimes eating normally but often refusing to eat. He hated to be alone and would jump out of a field or, if shut in a stable, sweat and tremble horribly.

The first problem was to reduce his weight without straining his heart or tendons. He ran away when ridden or lunged, so he was left loose beside a ridden horse, when he walked along meekly. Later he was ridden on a lead rein by small children, and finally ridden alone. Bitting, after several different attempts, was finally solved his way, for it was the only way that worked: he was given a fat, soft rubber bit and allowed to put his tongue over it. This unconventional solution raised many eyebrows, but he was controllable in it and accepted being bridled. Happier, he stopped running away so much. For years he was not caught in the field; instead, he followed the other horses into the yard, and was caught between them. He was well rewarded for this, and later could be caught on the way to the yard and finally in the field itself. Whenever he refused his food it was changed, or titbits added, until his appetite steadied.

Mangas was a bold, clean and educated jumper at home, but in early competitions he would not even get close enough to the first jump to qualify for a refusal. He was soon recognized from an old photograph as an ex-Wembley winner gone very sour. But he became a superb gymkhana pony and graduated to jumping cross-country (at first in pairs) and finally to occasional show-jumping again. By this time he was successful as a pony club type and he was virtually normal, though always a 'hot' character, competitive and great-hearted.

By Dollard and Miller's criteria Mangas was certainly neurotic: he was miserable, he had bad physical symptoms, and he was sometimes stupid. (Early on he leaped off a mountainside with me when refusing to leave other horses, and we both fell a clear 30 feet before hitting the ground. That is stupid.) Pavlov would have called him choleric, though he was never vicious, only violent. The cause of his neurosis certainly lay in his overexposure to jumping, the methods that had been used having created a constant conflict between his fear of hitting the jump and fear of being punished for refusal. (Even at home he would never approach a jump if anyone was standing by it: he knew what rapping was.) His hatred of the bit drove him to run away; again the methods used on him had made the problem worse. His return to normality took four years and a good deal of careful thought; had he been younger, or less neurotic, we might have treated him differently. I would say that he would break down again if subjected to the pressures of competitive jumping, but he is much admired and leads a useful life without having to be subjected to that. He was sold as a child's pony.

Emma was a beautiful 15.1 Arab-cob cross, raised on a farm where she was not handled but saw people regularly and had no fear of them. As a four-year-old she was caught for the first time, tied up (to 'teach her respect for the rope') and, when she had stopped fighting, lunged from a bit. As she seemed quiet, the farmer saddled and backed her on the fourth day; she stood for a second, then bucked him off and, screaming, broke several of his bones by jumping on him – an extraordinarily vicious and unnatural action.

When I bought her next morning Emma's head was skinned beneath the halter and her mouth grotesquely swollen. I led her ten miles home. For the first few miles she dragged behind like a beaten dog; then for about an hour she kept rushing up behind me and biting my back, which I ignored (the fatigue method!); and suddenly she stopped dead, insisted on smelling me all over, realized I was different, and trotted happily beside me. She never bit again, though she did pull dreadful faces that seemed to signify doubt rather than threat.

Emma's trauma left her terrified of three things: being ridden, her mouth, and men, but it also made her afraid of anything people did in general although she was bold enough when free. She was a timid horse, freezing when afraid, and inhibited in her action unless confident; she needed constant reassurance and praise. She was rebroken without being lunged, in a relaxed, almost casual manner, and gave no trouble although her tendency to tense up made it a lengthy process. She was not bitted but ridden on a sheepskin noseband, in which she was completely controllable; she competed successfully in local shows, and even small children gym-khana'ed her like that. She became an excellent teaching horse, for she slowed down whenever her rider was afraid, unbalanced, or too rough, but moved out well with a bold and sensitive rider. At first she was terrified of men, and several times attacked strangers walking across her field; but she did not mind boys, and we introduced her to older and older ones until she accepted young men, though she always retained an uncanny way of recognizing farmers.

Such trauma leaves a deep scar, and it is easy to become over-confident after a few months of success and allow a relapse which destroys all that carefully nurtured trust. *Zena*, a TB/quarter horse, was nearly Emma's double in temperament and history. She too would freeze when afraid, and had that typical inhibited action. She had been broken by an old cowboy, who had ridden her several times before she suddenly threw a fit and bucked him off. A series of bronc-busters had been hired to sort her out, but none of them stayed on her for more than a few seconds and she rapidly became an 'unbreakable' bronc. She was turned out for a year and not touched. I learned this story with some surprise, for I had just ridden her bareback to a new field in a halter. I rode her casually and bareback at first but then with increasing demands, until after several months she was schooled and jumping well. Only twice did she threaten to buck, both times from resentment at not being allowed to race horses galloping by, but she found her energies rapidly diverted. When I left I felt that although her progress had been steady and she was relaxed and responsive she was by no means totally recovered, and so recommended she should only be ridden by a girl, the gentler the better; but they put a cowboy on her just to make sure. . . . She was never ridden again.

Maestoso Sitnica III's problems arose from neither neurotic fear nor trauma, but sheer determination to escape pressure. A Lipizzan stallion, bold, vigorous and well-balanced, he was bred in Yugoslavia. As a nine-year-old he went to Germany as a dressage horse and was trained in a highly reputable stable. He then went to France, to Belgium, and finally to England. On the way he acquired a reputation for being extremely difficult to handle, although he was always with the best of trainers. He would not be caught in the box, would not be bridled, could not be led nor mounted. He knocked people down, ran over them, crashed through barriers and created havoc. He had no fear of, nor respect for, anything. The scars and lumps on his head bear testimony to the efforts made to control him.

Despite his breeding and training he was good for nothing but meat, for he was dangerous. At one time, when he was at stud and tantalized by the comings and goings of 'his' mares, he even became a vicious biter, though that was a short-lived phase. He was so explosive it was difficult to exercise him, and he could not be turned out as he had no respect for fences and could jump well. He could run away in almost any bit, and if he was stopped he simply did a series of courbettes followed by a ballotade instead. He went completely berserk when asked to back.

When he arrived he was given a huge, airy barn with a grand view, and a donkey jenny and several pigs for company. As he had been shut up in the dark alone for three months this interested and cheered him considerably. He was hand-fed throughout the day until he came to be caught. When ridden at first he had to be mounted in the box, then released to courbette across the hillside; he was always ridden in company, or he went off uncontrollably to look for some. At first everything was arranged in such a way that had he known my plans he would have wanted of his own accord to do what I was asking; this involved hiding my friends on mares at ever-increasing distances from his barn, and constant thought. Yet we made steady progress, and finally he came to believe that whatever I wanted to do must involve something good for him in the end, and he became patient, willing, and extremely interested in my ideas. He was also interested in the countryside, for he seemed to understand nothing about it; perhaps he had always been ridden indoors. He was always extraordinarily intelligent and alert.

After six months or so I found a place to school him, but when he realized what was happening he went berserk again, which surprised me: he had shown so clearly how well he understood his work that I had not realized his hatred of it. But with gradual rehabituation minutes of work built up to half an hour or more at a time, until he was once more what he was trained for, a superb dressage horse.

Maestoso liked to hack, fast, for at least two hours a day, preferably four. I once rode him a hundred miles in two days, carrying a load of gear, and he was fresh at the end of it: indeed, he insisted on a good ride the next day. Had that energy ever been fully tapped before? Or his intelligence?

Maestoso's problems stemmed from his immense strength, stamina and energy, coupled with unbending pride. Met by a domineering attitude and relentless overtraining, these made him violent and dangerous, as if he felt he were fighting for his life. After two or three years of exercise and freedom – he spent his summers on the mountain with a bunch of mares – his remarkable gentleness and nobility made it almost impossible to believe he was the same horse. That people with the technical skill and expertise to train him so beautifully should have had so little understanding of his psychic needs is a great sadness. Indeed, for him it was nearly a tragedy. It is in an effort to alleviate such sadnesses by directing attention to the science of horse behaviour, which we can expand and deepen as we have done equine veterinary science, that this book is written.

9

Where do we go from here?

'There is much talk of the misery which we cause to the brute creation; but they are recompensed by existence. If they were not useful to man, and therefore protected by him, they would not be nearly so numerous.' But the question is, whether the animals who endure such sufferings of various kinds, for the service and entertainment of man, would accept of existence upon the terms on which they have it.

(Boswell, quoting Dr Johnson in his *Life of Johnson*)

We have seen how a study of horse behaviour can lead us to understand their signals and achieve greater harmony with them; how we can use their social behaviour and our learning theory to train them more easily and pleasantly; and how we can understand their problems better. But a thoughtful reader cannot fail to have been struck by the stress that we so often place upon them in our insistence on keeping them in such unnatural conditions and doing such unnatural things with them. In the past a good deal of time has been spent on understanding and perfecting ways of looking after the horse's body, but remarkably little attention has been paid to his mind until it got in the way. It is surely time we gave a higher priority to a real understanding of that mentality. How many more panic-stricken horses must die before we design trailers that suit them?

At the moment, the 'high standards' of care that most of us have been taught to admire include spotless stables, artificial feeding, partial isolation, and imprisonment. Horses have very different ideas. Palatial dwellings are of no use to them. Their behaviour has evolved to meet the conditions of the wide open spaces, those of freedom, friendship, and a rich and varied life. Now it may not be possible to keep them in the conditions they would choose, but to reduce the stresses on them we can consider, item by item, what is lacking in their lives compared to that horse-Utopia of theirs, and make amends or substitutions. It may mean swallowing our pride from time to time, putting up with fat bellies and scruffier coats, but if we are true horse lovers we take more pride in happiness than appearances. A more natural system of horse care is not only beneficial to the horse's mental health but to his physical health too; it is easier; behaviour problems do not arise; and the vet's bills fall dramatically. Armed with a better knowledge of the horse's signals, we can look again at the horses around us, and we may find we change our views of whom and what we admire.

There is also a need for us to be working with their nature rather than against it. Again, at the moment show jumping is held in high esteem; but the number of horses that go 'sour' show that only those trainers with a true appreciation of the horse's mentality can develop a working relationship and sustain the horse's courage and interest. Such relationships are a delight to watch; but they are founded on knowledge and respect which may be beyond the reach of less patient, less sensitive, or more ambitious riders. For the less talented, is it not time that we started evolving new forms of competition (if compete we must) that suit horses better? The growing popularity of long-distance rides which, carefully controlled by vets' inspections, do not cause physical distress, is perhaps an indication that we are beginning to realize this need. Do these horses go sour and refuse to compete? To be honest I do not know, but I should very much doubt it: exploring along a well-dunged trail, perhaps in company, is an activity close to a horse's heart. Despite being badly ridden, our ponies on the whole have a better life than our horses since they seem not only more obdurate by nature but also more frightening when they do object because of the danger to our children: we are far more careful to choose conditions and activities that suit them, and so have developed many forms of competition that could surely be extended to the adult world of horses.

The desire to compete or to show off a horse we are proud of is not a base one, yet the conventions of the show ring again condemn many horses to an artificial, unsatisfactory life, to the detriment of their behaviour. 'Hunters' that would be lethal on a hunting field, 'hacks' that could not be hacked across country, and children's ponies that are dangerous until exercised for an hour by the groom, are only too commonly the winners in the show ring. Most of them would do their job cheerfully if suitably kept. But show ring standards demand that they are confined and overfed, and conventions are such that it has become positively insulting for a judge to be shown a horse *au naturel*. Can our judges really not evaluate the conformation of a whiskered horse in pasture condition? I think that they can, and that in the interests of the animals' mental health we should start changing our conventions and show them real horses instead of dotty dollies.

The keeping of stud stallions, and their handling and breeding, is another case. Many of us, in picking a stallion for our mare, would be likely to be more impressed by a fiery shiny creature bounding out of his box than a muddy chap sauntering after his mares, whatever the quality of his conformation; and in consequence we often let our mares in for some dreadful experiences, and ourselves in for dreadful bills.

I do not mean to denigrate all show jumpers, nor all stud owners, nor all those in the show ring, for there are many people and horses in these spheres who have found ways of overcoming the stresses, and there are many others in different spheres who create stresses just as great. It is the study of horse behaviour that has led me to notice these stresses, and to see that the greater they are the more skill it takes to overcome them, and the greater the incidence of failure. Most people who have dealt with horses for any length of time have been hurt by them sooner or later, and a surprising number have been killed, especially in racing stables. It is difficult to get true statistics on this point, for most give 'horse-related' casualties that include riding falls as well as attacks from demented horses; but in one survey of all causes of death (including car accidents, heart attacks and other diseases) in California, veterinarians mentioned that 7.5 per cent of cases were killed by horses.

The needless mental cruelty that we impose on our horses is seldom deliberate, and often not thought of as such. Much of it arises because of pressure from our peers, who in turn were impressed by the ideas of their peers. But life has changed; so have attitudes; and our knowledge is ever expanding. We are more aware of ourselves as being merely one species on the face of this planet rather than the End of Creation, and we have ceased to think that everything on this earth was put there for our amusement. Yet even those to whom the humanitarian aspects of better horse treatment do not appeal would do well to consider the problems for the sake of their own skins, and to reflect that an unhappy horse does not, and can not, do his best.

These are my own conclusions, drawn from my own experience and study. Some may find them hard to accept. I can only invite them to read the evidence – which is not my own, but the result of scientific investigation – and go out and look with fresh eyes, and come to their own conclusions. The horses cannot fail to benefit.

Appendix 1

A Pilot Study of the Mouthing Response

Menna Cooper-Willis

Introduction

The mouthing reaction is an easily identifiable response common to all young ponies. It is shown on meeting another pony and involves a snapping motion of the jaws. This may continue for some time with the ears held sideways to the head, which is usually extended forwards.

The study of this particular piece of behaviour was undertaken to try to find out a bit about its meaning and purpose. In most cases it is an all–or–none reaction and therefore we can get some idea of what cues ponies attend to when meeting other ponies.

The mouthing reaction (see page 73)

Method

In each case one pony was introduced to the experimental pony by leading both round the corner of a building or a wall, so that they could not see or smell each other before they met. Both animals were held loosely on halters. We tried to allow sufficient time (several hours) between each introduction, but in some cases habituation was probably involved.

In some cases we blindfolded one or both ponies to try to find out what cues they were attending to.

Results

The ponies used are listed below in order of age.

Number	Name	Age	Sex	Height	Type
1	Dick	25	gelding	13.2	Cob
2	Muffin	17	gelding[1]	11.3	Welsh sec. A
3	Tess	13	mare*	14.2	Irish cob (part Shire)
4	Betsan	10	mare	13.0	Welsh sec. C
5	Prince	9	gelding[1]	11.2	Welsh sec. A
6	Limerick	8	gelding	14.3	Riding pony
7	Llwydyn	4	gelding	13.0	Welsh sec. B
8	Seren	4	mare	13.0	Welsh sec. C
9	Josephine	3½	mare	13.2	Welsh sec. D
10	Hawk	3½	mare	11.2	Welsh sec. A
11	Sunshine	3½	gelding	12.2	Welsh sec. A
12	Anna	2½	filly	13.3	Part bred Arab
13	Sara	2½	filly*	12.1	Welsh sec. A
14	Twm	1½	colt	13.0	Part bred Arab
15	Dan	1½	rig	13.2	Cob
16	Oliver	1½	rig	13.1	Riding pony
17	Arthur	7 months	filly	11.2	Welsh cob foal (Josephine's, weaned)
18	Dinky	2½	jenny*	9.2	Donkey

* in foal;

[1] both these geldings show stallion-like behaviour and could be rigs, or proud-cut (common in this type) or merely cut late.

Numbers 10, 14, 15, 16 and 17 were used as experimental animals by testing them against some, or all, of the others. Number 10 was used as an experimental animal because she was the same size and colour as the foal, though older.

A   Reactions of number 10 (Hawk)

Test animal	Observations
1 (Dick)	No contact for 20 seconds. Sniffed noses. No other reaction.
6 (Limerick)	Ignored each other after sniffing noses.
16 (Oliver)	Ignored each other after sniffing noses.
18 (Dinky)	Hawk was alarmed at the sight of Dinky, who did not put her ears back. After sniffing noses Hawk was more alarmed and withdrew.

B   Reactions of number 14 (Twm)

Test Animal	Observations
3 (Tess)	Tess had her ears back and tail lashing as Twm approached. Tess then charged him and he withdrew.
4 (Betsan)	Sniffed noses and Betsan moved her ears around a lot. Then they sniffed each other's shoulders and Betsan slowly turned her back on him.
7 (Llwydyn)	Sniffed noses very carefully for some time with both their heads low. Llwydyn squealed suddenly and struck out with a forefoot: Twm withdrew.
8 (Seren)	Sniffed each other's shoulders carefully for 15 seconds. Both ponies put their ears back and Seren lashed her tail slightly. Then sniffed each other's noses and made no other reaction.
9 (Josephine)	Josephine had her ears back and tail lashing as Twm approached. He sniffed her nose briefly and withdrew.
10 (Hawk)	Sniffed noses very carefully. Hawk then squealed and struck out with a forefoot. Twm jumped back and Hawk turned her rump on him quickly.
11 (Sunshine)	Approached each other keenly, sniffed each other's shoulders and then sniffed noses. Twm then sniffed Sunshine's foreleg and shoulders and bit him (hard) on the withers. (N.B. not mutual grooming bite)
12 (Anna)	Anna was eating grass as she approached. Sniffed noses for a few seconds. Anna resumed eating and Twm turned away and pawed.

C   Reactions of number 15 (Dan)

Test animal	Mouthing	Observations
3 (Tess)	Yes	Tess had her ears back and tail lashing. Immediate mouthing from Dan.
9 (Josephine)	No	Josephine had her ears back and tail lashing. Sniffed noses.

11 (Sunshine)	Yes	Dan would not approach Sunshine, but immediately began mouthing. When Sunshine approached he went on mouthing and ran away.
12 (Anna)	No	Sniffed noses.
12 (Anna)	Yes	Dan mouthed slightly. (*See discussion*)

D   Reactions of number 16 (Oliver)

Test animal	Mouthing	Observations
1 (Dick)	No	Sniffed noses carefully for some time, then both withdrew.
2 (Muffin)	Yes	Both approached with ears forward and sniffed noses. Muffin squealed slightly, Oliver put one ear back and they then sniffed each other's shoulders. Muffin bit Oliver's shoulder, whereupon Oliver began mouthing but soon stopped. They went on sniffing shoulders and the same thing happened again.
3 (Tess)	Yes	Tess charged towards him with her ears back, tail lashing and teeth exposed. Oliver mouthed immediately, jumped backwards and stopped mouthing. He would not go near Tess and when she tried to attack him again he started mouthing.
9 (Josephine)	Yes	Reactions of both like those above.
10 (Hawk)	Yes	They sniffed noses; after 15 seconds Hawk snapped at him. Oliver immediately began mouthing.
11 (Sunshine)	Yes	Sniffed noses for 10–15 seconds, with both ponies' ears forward. Oliver mouthed feebly but soon stopped, and both continued sniffing.
12 (Anna)	Yes	Sniffed noses, Oliver began mouthing, and Anna squealed.
13 (Sara)	Yes	Sara put her ears back when she saw him, and Oliver immediately began mouthing. Sara sniffed his nose as he tried to withdraw. Sara then withdrew, ears still back.
13 (Sara)	No	(Both ponies blindfolded.) Sniffed noses, both moving their ears back and forth.
13 (Sara)	No	(Sara blindfolded.) Oliver reluctant to approach. Both moving their ears around.

		Sara put her ears back but Oliver took no notice. She then flattened her ears and head thrust at him, and Oliver turned away. She snapped slightly but Oliver ignored her.
13 (Sara)	Yes	Oliver reluctant to approach. Sara came at him with her ears back and head thrust at him. No reaction from Oliver. They sniffed noses and Sara put her ears back and head thrust at him, teeth exposed. Oliver mouthed slightly.
3 (Tess)	Yes	Oliver sniffed Tess's nose, Tess put her ears back, exposed her teeth and lashed her tail. Oliver mouthed immediately.
3 (Tess)	Yes	(Tess blindfold.) Tess put her ears back and lashed her tail on catching a whiff of Oliver. He would not make contact. When she showed her teeth he mouthed slightly and withdrew.
3 (Tess)	Yes	(Tess blindfold.) Oliver sniffed her just out of contact with his ears forward. When Tess smelled him she flattened her ears, lashed her tail, exposed her teeth and tried to bite him. He mouthed and withdrew.
18 (Dinky)	No	Sniffed noses with their ears forward. Dinky jerked her nose at him with her ears back and he withdrew.

E Reactions of number 17 (*Arthur*)

Test Animal	Mouthing	Observations
1 (Dick)	Yes	Arthur immediately mouthed and they sniffed noses.
2 (Muffin)	Yes	Arthur immediately mouthed and nuzzled Muffin, still mouthing. Muffin squealed loudly.
3 (Tess)	Yes	Arthur immediately mouthed and Tess turned away, ears back.
4 (Betsan)	Yes	Arthur immediately mouthed and Betsan put her ears back, forward and back again.
6 (Limerick)	Yes	Sniffed noses and Arthur then began mouthing.
7 (Llwydyn)	Yes	Arthur immediately mouthed and Llwydyn advanced, ears forward.

8 (Seren)	No	Sniffed noses. No mouthing from Arthur. (Habituation?)
10 (Hawk)	Yes	Arthur immediately mouthed and Hawk ignored her.
11 (Sunshine)	Yes	Prolonged mouthing from Arthur. Both withdrew, then Arthur barged into Sunshine, ears back, and Sunshine tried to flee.
13 (Sara)	Yes	Sara's ears were back. Arthur immediately mouthed but Sara lunged forward with ears back, head forward and teeth exposed.
14 (Twm)	Yes	Immediate mouthing from Arthur. Twm ignored her.
15 (Dan)	Yes	Immediate mouthing from Arthur.
16 (Oliver)	Yes	Sniffed noses and Arthur then mouthed slightly.
18 (Dinky)	Yes	Arthur hesitant on approaching; Dinky's ears forward. They sniffed noses, Dinky put her ears back and Arthur immediately started mouthing. Dinky approached, ears back, and Arthur fled.

Discussion

By 'experimental animal' we mean the animal in which the mouthing reaction is being tested, and by 'test animal' we mean the pony that the experimental animal is tested against.

1. Arthur showed mouthing to all test animals (except Sara, where habituation was suspected as she had been introduced to 4 animals within about 10 minutes). From other observations one would suspect that foals of this age always show mouthing. Arthur has been seen doing it to strange foals, though not in this experiment.

2. The three yearlings showed great individual differences. Twm showed no mouthing. He tended to sniff the ponies carefully, often sniffing their shoulders.

Dan, a rig, showed some mouthing. In the order that they were done the tests went as follows:

	Josephine	Anna	Tess	Sunshine	Anna
mouthing:	no	no	yes	yes	yes

We felt that the last two positive reactions were influenced by his reaction to Tess. He was scared by her and was then more careful of later ones. This was the first indication that mouthing is given as a submissive gesture in response to aggression.

Oliver mouthed to most ponies but usually not until the other pony showed aggression. As he got more bored it took more aggressive behaviour to make him mouth: first ears back; then ears back and head thrust; then ears back and head thrust and teeth exposed.

3. Our results led us to conclude that mouthing is a submissive gesture but we are uncertain whether the gesture has any effect on the aggression of the test animals, since they often went on attacking. Zeeb suggested that mouthing developed into mutual grooming in older animals but we found no evidence of this.

4. From blindfolding we found that the sight of a large pony was not enough to make an older experimental animal start mouthing, nor was the smell. (*See* Oliver's tests with Sara and Tess.) However, when Tess became aggressive mouthing did begin. When the test animals were blindfolded we saw that it was not just the sight of the experimental animal that had made them aggressive – it was the smell.

Degrees of aggressive response

From observation we decided that there are different degrees of aggression which are ordered:

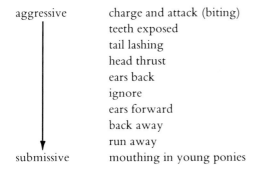

aggressive	charge and attack (biting)
	teeth exposed
	tail lashing
	head thrust
	ears back
	ignore
	ears forward
	back away
	run away
submissive	mouthing in young ponies

The mares tended to be more aggressive than the geldings, and there are great individual differences in aggressiveness. In a group the bosses tend to be the larger, older animals (e.g., Tess and Josephine). Aggression towards other ponies seems to have no connection with aggression towards people.

Very young animals show mouthing to all other ponies. We suggest that as the pony gets older it takes a higher degree of aggression to release the mouthing response. This also appears to differ with individuals (e.g., differences between Twm and Oliver). Because of the small numbers in the experiment we cannot tell whether this is due to inherent character differences or whether it is due to their different stages of maturity. Although they are the same age and both are entire Twm is extremely well-grown and has fully descended testes whereas Oliver is very undergrown and his testes are undescended. Dan is somewhere between the two in maturity.

Appendix 2

Opportunities for Further Study

1. *Experiments at home* For some reason, behaviour studies on domestic animals have never been popular with scientists: we know more about the behaviour of gorillas and chaffinches than horses and dogs. But single observations on single horses, however interesting, usually tell us little about general behaviour patterns. What is needed are studies that follow the basic principles of any research:

(a) Have a clear idea in your mind about what it is that you are trying to find out.

(b) Try to sort out the likely causes of the effects you notice, and test them one by one. Write down the test conditions, so that you or anyone else can repeat the tests, for they are useless if they cannot be repeated.

(c) Use as many animals as possible, so that one horse's oddities do not confuse the general picture.

(d) Keep careful notes, including things you may not think relevant at the time, for example, age, breed, sex, weather, whether a mare is in season or not. Many discoveries have been made by people who started out thinking that one thing affected another, only to find that it was a third, unsuspected cause that was producing the effect. Moreover, when everything is recorded it often becomes possible to use the results in another experiment.

(e) Don't ignore negative results! Only too often people become convinced of an idea because they only count the number of times it works, and never the times that it doesn't.

(f) Occam's razor. Don't believe in causes that aren't necessary. I personally don't believe in telepathy between people and horses because as far as I can see horses are perfectly sensitive enough to be able to see from his movements what is going on in somebody's mind.

(g) Do not be depressed by the fact that you will almost certainly end up with more questions than you started out with: that is a hallmark of good research, and its great fascination.

Moyra Williams' book *Horse Psychology* gives a number of examples of simple tests, done at home, which gave her great insight into the horse's mind.

Appendix 1 is a study of foal behaviour done by a 15-year-old, very simply, with her friends' borrowed ponies. Nobody else had studied 'mouthing' and hers are the only clear-cut results that we have. As serious scientific research it would be found lacking: she had no stopwatch, relatively few animals, and sometimes had to interfere with the results lest the ponies hurt each other. Nevertheless she found out a great deal (including the 'threat series' which at the time had not been described). The results are detailed enough to be analysed in different ways, or to be used in other studies ... and they gave rise to numerous other, testable, questions.

2. The Equine Behaviour Study Circle is a British group with US links which holds meetings and talks, and publishes a bi-annual newsletter of members' contributions. Further details from: Mrs Gillian Hemsworth (also known as Susan McBane), 9 Rostherne Avenue, Lowton St Luke's, Warrington, or The Hon. Mrs Moyra Williams, Leyland Farm, Gawcott, Bucks. The Circle would be interested in the results of any behavioural studies (and so would I).

3. Aberystwyth University offers an MSc course in Equine Studies, which is not specifically a behaviour course although there is opportunity for research.

4. Dr Marthe Kiley-Worthington, Milton Court, Polegate, Sussex, who has been doing research on horse behaviour for many years, runs an advisory service on behavioural problems in horses (and other farm animals). She also takes students for BHSAI and NPS diplomas. Behavioural research is done at the farm and training in experimental procedure, observation, recording and analysis of data is given.

Recommended Further Reading

Ledbetter, Bonnie, and Tom Ainslie, *The Body Language of Horses* (Morrow, New York, 1980)
   Well-founded personal observations. No illustrations.
Podhajsky, Alois, *The Complete Training of Horse and Rider in the Principles of Classical Horsemanship* (Wilshire Books, California, 1975)
   Even for those not particularly interested in dressage, the wisdom and attitudes of the Director of the Spanish Riding School in Vienna are invaluable.
Ryden, Hope, *Mustangs: a Return to the Wild* (Penguin, 1978)
Schafer, Michael, *The Language of the Horse* (Kaye and Ward, 1974)
   Excellent and thoughtful observations, with photographs.
Self, Margaret Cabell, *The Problem Horse and the Problem Horseman* (Arco, 1977)
   Sound practical advice.
Vavra, Robert, *Such is the Real Nature of Horses* (Collins, 1979)
   Superb colour photographs, with explanatory commentary, of social behaviour in free-ranging Spanish and Camargue horses, with an unfortunate emphasis on aggression.
Williams, Moyra, *Horse Psychology* (Allen, 1976)
   A psychologist's thoughts and experiments on her own horses. Lacks illustrations.

Bibliography

Archer, M., 'Species preferences of grazing horses', *J. Brit. Grassland Soc. 28* (1973), 123

Ardrey, Robert, *The Social Contract* (Collins, 1970)

Baer, K. L., 'Observations on learning in horses', *J. Anim. Sci. 49 (1979) Suppl. 1*

Barth, R., 'Colic in horses', *Inaugural Dissertation, Ludwig-Maximilians Universitat* (1980)

Berger, J., 'Organizational systems and dominance in feral horses in the Grand Canyon', *Behav. Ecol. Sociobiol. 2* (1977), 91-119

Bernstein, I. S., 'Dominance: the baby and the bathwater', *Behav. and Brain Sci.* (1961)

Bobylev, I., 'Study of the typological features in the higher nervous activity of performance horses,' *Konevodstvo i Konnyi Sport 2* (1960), 19. (In Russian only.)

Boy, Vincent, and Patrick Duncan, 'Time-budgets of Camargue horses', 1. *Behav. 71* (1979) (3-4), 187-202; 2. *Behav. 72* (1980) (1-2), 26-49

Chance, M. R. A., 'Attention structure as the basis of primate rank orders', *Man,* (Dec. 1967)

Chenevix-Trench, Charles, *A History of Horsemanship* (Doubleday, 1970)

Chuang-Tzu, Trans. Herbert Giles (Allen & Unwin, 1980)

Clabby, John, *Natural History of Horses* (Taplinger, New York, 1976)

Clutton-Brock, T. H., P. J. Greenwood, and R. D. Powell, 'Ranks and relationships in highland ponies', *Z. Tierpsychol. 41* (1976), 202-206

Cox, J., *Equine Vet. Rev.,* 25 (1979), 86

Darwin, C., *Expression of the Emotions in Man and Animals* (Greenwood Press, 1868)

Dixon, J. C., 'Pattern discrimination, learning set and memory in a pony', *Thoroughbred Record 192* (1970)

Dollard, J. C., and N. E. Miller, *Personality and Psychotherapy* (McGraw-Hill, New York, 1950)

Dubos, Rene, 'Humanistic biology', *Amer. Scientist 53* (1965), 4-19

Duncan, P., and N. Vigne, 'Effects of group size in horses on the rate of attacks by bloodsucking flies', *Anim. Behav. 27* (1979), 623-625

Esser, A. H. (Ed.), *Behaviour and Environment* (MacBride/Plenum, 1971)

Evans, W., A. Borton, H. Hintz, and van Vleck (Eds), *The Horse* (Freeman, San Francisco, 1977)

Fagen, R. M., and T. K. George, 'Play behaviour and exercise in young ponies', *Behav. Ecol. Sociobiol. 2* (1977), 267

Feist, J.D., and D.R. McCullough, 'Behaviour patterns and communications in feral horses', *Z. Tierpsychol. 41* (1976), 337–371

Fiske, J.C., *How Horses Learn* (Stephen Greene, Vermont, 1979)

———— and G. D. Potter, 'Discrimination reversal learning in yearling horses', *J. Anim. Sci. 49* (1979) (2)

Fox, M. W., (Ed.), *Abnormal Behaviour in Animals* (Saunders, 1968)

Fraser, A. F., 'Behaviour disorders in domestic animals', *See Fox* (1968)

———— *Reproductive Behaviour in Ungulates* (Academic Press, 1968)

Gann, Shiela, MSc Thesis, Equine Studies, Aberystwyth (1981)

Gardner, L. P., 'Responses of horses in a discrimination problem', *J. Comp. Physiol. Psychol. 23* (1937), 13

·———— 'Responses of horses to the same signal in different positions', *J. Comp. Physiol. Psychol. 23*, 304 (1937)

Grzimek, B., 'Versuche über das Farbsehn von Pflanzenessern 1. Das farbige Sehn (und die Sehrscharfe) von Pferden', *Z. Tierpsychol. 9* (1950), 23

———— 'Colour vision in horses', *Z. Tierpsychol. 11* (1952), 23

Hafez, E. S. E., *Behaviour of Domestic Animals* (Balliere, Tindall, Cox, London, 1975)

Hamilton, S., 'Synchronising horse and man', *Equus 21* (1981), 26

Hediger, H., *Studies in the Psychology and Behaviour of Animals in Zoos and Circuses* (Butterworths, 1955)

Hierd, J. C., A. M. Lennon, and R. W. Bell, 'Effects of early experience on the learning ability of yearling horses', *J. Anim. Sci. 53* (1981) 5

Hill, Winfred F., *Learning: a survey of Psychological Interpretations* (Chandler, 1971)

Horse Protection Regulations, U.S. Department of Agriculture, Animal and Plant Health Inspection Service

Houpt, K. A., Rudman, and Haag, 'Social dominance and learning in horses', *J. Anim. Sci. 50* (1980) (2)

———— and T. R. Wolski, 'Stability of equine hierarchies and the prevention of dominance-related aggression', *Equine Vet. J. 12* (1980) (I), 15

———— Equine practice 1 (1979)

Huxley, Julian, *Essays of a Humanist* (Harper & Row, 1964)

Ippolitova, T. V., 'Emotional stress in horses of different types of higher nervous activity', *Sbornik Nauchnykh Trudov Moskovskaya Vaterinarnaya Akademiya 100* (1978), 36 (In Russian only)

Kiley-Worthington, M., 'The vocalisations of ungulates, their causation and function', *Z. Tierpsychol. 31* (1972), 171

———— 'Tail movements of ungulates', *Behav. 56* (1976), 69–115

———— *Behavioural Problems of Farm Animals* (Oriel Press, 1977)

Klingel, H., 'Comparison of social behaviour of equidae' in V. Geist and F. Walther (eds), *The Behaviour of Ungulates and its Relation to Management*, Int. Symp. Univ. Calgary (IUCN Publ, 1974)

Knill, J., R. D. Eagleton and E. Harver, 'Physical optics of the equine eye', *Am. J. Vet. Res. 38* (1977), 735

Kurtsin, I. T., 'Experimental neurosis in dogs' (*See Fox*)

Lao Tzu: Tao te Ching *in* Arthur Waley, *The Way and its Power* (Allen & Unwin, 1934)

Mader, D. R., and E. O. Price, 'Discrimination learning in horses: effects of breed, age and social dominance', *J. Anim. Sci.* 50 (1980) (5)

Masserman, J. H., *Behaviour and Neurosis: an Experimental Psychoanalytic Approach* (Univ. Chicago Press, 1943)

McCall, C. A., G. D. Potter, T. H. Friend, and R. S. Ingram, 'Learning abilities in yearling horses using the Hebb-Williams closed field maze', *J. Anim. Sci. 53* (1981) (4)

Miller, J., and R. H. Denniston, 'Interband dominance in feral horses', *Z. Tierpsychol. 51* (1979) (1), 41

Odberg, F., and K. F. Smith, 'Study on eliminative and grazing behaviour', *Equine Vet. J. 8* (1976), 147

Popov, N. F., 'Characteristics of higher nervous activity of horses', *Zh. Vyssh. Nervn. Deiatel* (J. higher nervous activity, Pavlov. Inst.) 6 (1956), 718

Potter, G. and B. F. Yeates, 'Behavioural principles of training and management', in *The Horse* (*See Evans*)

Prince, Dominic, and J. Beer, 'Knowing the head case', *Pacemaker* (1982) Nov.

Rossdale, P. D., 'Perinatal behaviour in the thoroughbred horse' (*See Fox*)

———— *The Horse* (J. A. Allen, 1975)

Rowell, T. E., 'Social dominance', *Behav. Biol. 11* (1974), 131

Rowlands, I. W., 'Horse fertility', *Equine Vet. J. 13* (1981) (2), 85

Rubenstein, D. I., 'Behavioural ecology of island feral horses (Shackleford Banks)', *Equine Vet. 13* (1981)

Rubin, L., C. Oppegard, and H. F. Hintz, 'Effect of varying temporal distribution of conditioning trials on equine learning behaviour', *J. Anim. Sci. 50* (1980) (6)

Ruckebusch, Y., 'The relevance of drowsiness in the circadian cycle of farm animals', *Anim. Behav. 20* (1972), 637

Sadleir, *Ecology of Reproduction in Wild and Domestic Animals* (Methuen, 1969)

Schoen, A. M. S., E. M. Banks, and S. E. Curtis, 'Behaviour of young Shetland and Welsh ponies', *Biol. Behav. 1* (1976), 192

Sereni, M. L., and M. F. Bouisseau, 'Use of a food competition method as an indicator for dominance relationships in horses', *Biol. Behav. 3* (1978), 87

Sivak, J., and J. G. Allen, 'An evaluation of the ramp retina of the horse eye', *Vision Res. 15* (1975), 1353

Smyth, R. H., *The Mind of the Horse* (J. A. Allen, 1974)

Summerhays, R. S., *The Problem Horse* (J. A. Allen, 1959)

Tembrock, G., 'Communication in Ungulates', in T. A. Sebeok, *Animal Communication*, p. 388 (Indiana Univ. Press, 1968)

Toates, F. M., *Animal Behaviour – a Systems Approach* (John Wiley, 1980)

Thorpe, W. H., *Animal Nature and Human Nature* (Anchor/Doubleday, 1974)

Tyler, S. J., 'Behaviour and Social organisation of New Forest ponies', *Anim. Behav.* (1972), Monograph 5, 2

Valdez, H. 'Perforating gastrointestinal ulcers in foals', *Equine Practice 1* (1979) (5), 44

Veeckman, J. L., and F. Odberg, *Vlaans diergeneeskundig tijdschift 47* (1978) (3)

Washburn, S. L., and D. Hamburg, in de Vore, Irven: *Primate Behaviour* (Holt, Rinehart & Winston, 1965)

Wells, S. M., 'Social behaviour and relationships in a herd of Camargue ponies', *Z. Tierpsychol. 49* (1979) (4), 363

Welsh, D. A., 'The life of Sable Island wild horses', *Can. Nat.* 7 (1973)

Xenophon, trans. Morris H. Morgan, *The Art of Horsemanship* (J. A. Allen)

Young, J. Z., *Programs of the Brain* (Oxford University Press, 1978)

Index

Page numbers in italic refer to the illustrations and captions